ENERGY SECRETS
For Tired
Mothers On The Run

B. Kaye Olson

Health Communications, Inc.
Deerfield Beach, Florida

Library of Congress Cataloging-in-Publication Data

Olson, B. Kaye
    Energy secrets for tired mothers on the run / B. Kaye Olson.
      p. cm.
    Includes bibliographical references.
    ISBN 1-55874-250-6 : $11.95
    1. Mothers — Health and hygiene. 2. Mothers — Time management. 3.
Mothers — Psychology. I. Title
RA564.85.O47 1993
613'.085'2—dc20   93-32930
                                                                          CIP

©1993 B. Kaye Olson
ISBN 1-55874-2506

Publisher: Health Communications, Inc.
              3201 S.W. 15th Street
              Deerfield Beach, FL 33442-8190

Cover design by Barbara Bergman

DEDICATION

To you, the mother:
May your life be healthier,
your relationships better and may
you have more energy because
you chose to read this book.

ACKNOWLEDGMENTS

Energy Secrets evolved with the support of several people. Special gratitude goes to Linda R. Peckham, professor of English, Lansing Community College, Lansing, Michigan. Her coaching, feedback and energy over the years made this book a reality.

Thanks to Judy McQueen, Suzanne Hollister Saltman and Laura Fawcett for their endless reading, feedback and support.

Recognition goes to Edward J. Madara, director of the American Self-Help Clearinghouse, for his assistance in providing state-by-state self-help clearinghouse information for the appendix.

Thanks to my daughters, Barbara Butts and Debra Meredith, for their support and without whom I could not have written a book for mothers. To my grandchildren, Zachary and Ashlee Butts, thank you for playing with me to balance out my hard work. To my husband, Erik Olson, thank you for the support along the journey. Special recognition goes to my grandmother, Nellie Annear, who always inspires and encourages me. To other family and friends who believe in this book, thank you.

Special thanks to Barbara Nichols, Peter Vegso and the Health Communications staff who made *Energy Secrets* a reality.

To all of the mothers I have worked with over the last 30 years, thank you for the inspiration. To today's mother anxiously awaiting this book, enjoy.

CONTENTS

INTRODUCTION

Many mothers today are exhausted. Their energy resources are depleted, yet they push themselves to work longer and harder than ever before. And still they put themselves down because they aren't achieving more.

Mothers are paying a high price for their compulsive striving to be superhuman. Guilt and anger siphon off their priceless energy. Their relationships are compromised, resulting in conflicts and breakups.

Their health is also jeopardized, not only by fatigue, but also by stress-related illnesses and disease. Burnout is a reality today as mothers neglect themselves and struggle to meet family and societal expectations.

Many mothers feel they want to start taking control of their lives again. They feel alone, overwhelmed with demands, out of balance. They are desperate for information on how they can feel better, re-energize themselves and become more stabilized.

Energy Secrets is the result of many years of my watching mothers become more stressed out, burned out and dysfunctional due to exhaustion. As a former nurse practitioner, and now a stress consultant and educator, with a B.A. in psychology and an M.A. in family studies, I have worked for over 30 years with hundreds of mothers and families regarding health and coping.

Because of my concern about the health of mothers, I designed and implemented a class in 1986 entitled "Preventing Parent Burnout" at

Lansing Community College, Lansing, Michigan. In addition to continuing to teach this course, I also give seminars and workshops to organizations and groups on balance, self-talk, family stress, empowerment, self-management and humor in the workplace.

This book is based on a simple premise that a mother's function is dependent on sufficient energy. Mothers are given ideas on how to find, pace, replenish and protect their energy resources.

I encourage introspection through numerous questions, exercises and self-inventories. Mothers are given many tips, skills and techniques to help them cope and take charge of their lives.

Motherhood stress and burnout potential are discussed first, followed by personality traits that block needed balance. Other topics include communication, time, self-talk, diet, exercise, sleep, chores, career and goals. Self-responsibility and ownership of choices are encouraged throughout the book.

The final chapter offers five building blocks for self-empowerment that provide mothers with the hope and belief that they can move themselves and their families in a healthy direction. Each chapter provides a summary model of information and health plus energy pointers for busy mothers on the run. The appendix has a state-by-state self-help clearinghouse list that can help mothers connect with an appropriate group.

Energy Secrets is for all mothers — tired mothers, mothers working through the steps of recovery or women who just want to feel better. Healthcare and helping professionals will also appreciate the practical and useful information, as will groups, agencies and institutions working with mothers, children and families.

This book is written for mothers who have a passion to learn, grow, develop and move forward in life. Empowerment, energy and health can be yours.

Let us begin.

1

Are You Fizzling Out?

**I choose to take control
of my life**

Tired? Out of energy? Do you feel too "pooped" to parent? Are you on a nonstop merry-go-round and can't get off? Do you dream of running away from it all?

Welcome to motherhood. These feelings are normal. They happen to all mothers. Millions of other women feel that way, too.

Stress is a little word that's overused and underestimated. The implications of chronic stress on today's mothers are shocking. This year millions of women will get sick because they refuse to slow down and *balance* their work with play.

Yet stress is essential to life. It can be positive. It motivates, stimulates, challenges and produces energy. Experts say you would be dead without stress, but how much stress?

Mothers function best with a moderate amount of stress. Your efficiency peaks with a reasonable number of demands, you are more organized and you perform better.

Think of a time in your life when you were bored, lacked structure and

1

your life had no stimulation. Perhaps it was before motherhood, or when you were laid off from a job. How productive were you at home? You may have been completely disorganized and inefficient. You may not have accomplished anything.

Now consider the other extreme. Think of a time when you were under excessive stress. The high stress level became chronic. You were on stress overload and could not meet the demands placed on you month after month. Eventually you became sick.

Rate your stress level over the past three months. Check one.

☐ Low ☐ Moderate ☐ High ☐ Excessive

If you checked high or excessive, list one small area in your life you want to change.

_____

How could you start to change?

_____

Problems mount when mothers are under intense pressure for too long, which is all too common today. Use the analogy of a car. You can drive a car into the ground, but the motor overheats and the cooling system fails. Cars don't run indefinitely. Neither do you. Constant pushing in *overdrive* backfires.

You can run out of energy and even collapse. The constant outpouring of stress chemicals such as adrenaline and cortisol can kill you. When your mind and body are overstressed, they rebel. They can tolerate only a certain amount of abuse before they scream ENOUGH! and shutdown occurs. It is only a matter of time.

Three-fourths of the women at a family doctor's office are there for stress-related problems: fatigue, backaches, menstrual irregularities, high blood pressure, arthritis, skin disorders, migraine headaches or irritable bowel syndrome.

Decide *now*. Is stress worth dying for? You *can* take charge of your life.

A Mother Knows When She Is Under Stress

She . . . drives the children to McDonald's, orders, pays and takes off without the food.

. . . opens the clothes dryer to remove the laundry and the cat jumps out.

. . . uses the men's restroom at the mall and doesn't realize it for 30 minutes.

You may relate to these incidents. Stress affects everyone. You will always be challenged by stress. There may be no such thing as a stressless life, but you can change the way you react to it.

Write one funny thing that happened to you when you were under high stress levels.

_____

_____

_____

Can you laugh about it now?

Listen To Yourself

Listen to your mind and body. They send you messages that you are under stress. Do you listen? Or do you deny those vital clues? Do you shift your motor into overdrive and push harder? *Not listening can be hazardous to your health.*

Identify Stress Signals

Identify your stress signals. This is important. Once you recognize your symptoms, you can choose to change the way you perceive a person or situation, intercept your reaction to an event or initiate coping skills.

Signals Of Burnout

What mental, emotional, physical and behavioral signs of stress do you exhibit? Read through the following columns of stress signals. Check each persistent symptom you have experienced in the past 6 months:

Mental/emotional

_____ irritability

_____ inability to concentrate

_____ forgetfulness

_____ increased anxiety

_____ anger

_____ excessive worrying

_____ increased crying

_____ other

Physical

_____ headaches

_____ fatigue

_____ stomach/bowel problems

_____ frequent colds

_____ shoulder/neck tension

_____ eating changes

_____ insomnia

_____ other

Behavioral

_____ short fuse

_____ substance abuse

_____ social withdrawal

_____ decreased sex drive

_____ increased drug use

_____ missed deadlines

_____ using people

_____ other

How many did you check? If you identified many symptoms, evaluate your stress levels *now.* You can make choices.

Review those checked symptoms again. Which ones are most intense? Most frequent? Most continuous?

List your three most intense, continuous signals.

_____

_____

_____

Mothers today are more vulnerable to burnout for several reasons:

- Society continues to program girls to be the major caretakers.
- More women are in the paid workforce.

- Women take on more and more major roles, refusing to relinquish others.
- Mothers continually strive to be superwomen.
- Single mothers pressure themselves to be two people.
- Mothers allow pervasive guilt to drive them into work overload.
- Male help in the home has increased, yet it remains deficient in many families.

What is burnout? It is a progressive movement toward mental, emotional, spiritual and physical exhaustion. It is insidious. It claims the most dedicated, committed and sensitive mothers. Very few mothers recognize they are drifting into burnout.

The cause of this debilitating syndrome is twofold:

1. Chronic stress overload
2. Energy deficit

Continuous stress overload will create energy deficiency.

Burnout occurs when demands for energy (output) chronically exceed restoration of energy reserves (input). You can be at high risk for burnout if you are a nonassertive "people pleaser." You can be more prone to burnout if you are idealistic and have unrealistic expectations of yourself and others. These qualities and behaviors drain you of energy.

If you've ever reached burnout, were contributing factors mostly mental, emotional, physical or behavioral?

How "Hot" Are You?

Read each statement below and score yourself using the following key:

1. never
2. sometimes
3. frequently
4. constantly

_____ I scream at the children over little things.

_____ People say I overreact.

_____ I snap at my family and relatives.

_____ Fatigue is an ongoing problem.

_____ Crying comes easily.

_____ Guilt runs my life.

_____ I feel trapped as a mother.

_____ Stress symptoms occur daily.

_____ My anger is out of control.

_____ I can't cope.

_____ Friends say I'm unsociable.

_____ I feel sad. I'm unhappy with the way things are.

_____ Alcohol, smoking or caffeine is a problem.

_____ I resent the children.

_____ Life seems meaningless.

_____ **Total your points.**

Scoring:

15-25 — Cool. No serious problem with burnout.

26-35 — Tepid. Evaluate your life now. Increase your awareness of stress and coping.

36-45 — Warm to very warm. Take action. Cut back on your workload and increase breaks to re-energize. Use coping techniques. Improve your nutrition, sleep and exercise. Consider counseling.

46-55 — Sizzling. Get professional help now. Reduce work hours immediately. Ask for help to get immediate relief. Increase sleep, good nutrition, breaks, exercise and play.

56-60 — Boiling point. Professional help and support are absolutes. You need a complete respite *now*.

What temperature are you?

_____

List one identified problem from this inventory that you would like to work on.

_____

_____

_____

Unrealistic Expectations

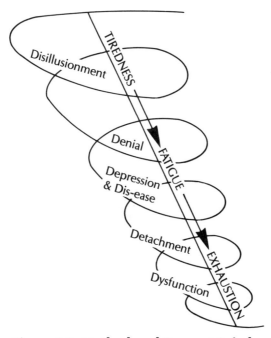

Figure 1.1. Motherhood Burnout Spiral

Prevent Burnout Through Awareness

You can prevent the debilitating syndrome of burnout by increasing your awareness of it. Visualize a spiral with five progressive stages:

1. disillusionment
2. denial
3. depression and dis-ease
4. detachment
5. dysfunction.

A common thread through the downward drift is tiredness, chronic fatigue, then exhaustion. (See Figure 1.1)

Dynamic enthusiasm precedes burnout. Some experts say you can't burn out unless you have been on fire. A mother can be overcommitted and overconsumed with parenting. She can have unrealistic expectations of parenthood. Overdedication and failure to take care of herself and to have outside interests can ease her into burnout.

STAGE 1. DISILLUSIONMENT

Disillusionment occurs when a mother's idealistic expectations cannot be met. She senses something is wrong, but she can't put her finger on it. Parenting isn't what she expected. Frustration and confusion set in.

STAGE 2. DENIAL

Denial is common. A mother ignores her feelings, and soon irritability and anger set in. Stress symptoms such as headaches, stomach problems or insomnia increase. She denies these signals and develops an "If only I try harder" attitude. Pushing harder compromises energy reserves and tiredness becomes her daily companion. Family relationships are strained.

Some mothers, aware of the energy void and increasing stress level, make powerful decisions. They cut back on their workload and increase coping skills, self-nurturing and sleep. This action can pull them out of the burnout process. Mothers in denial continue to drift downward.

STAGE 3. DEPRESSION AND DIS-EASE

Depression occurs. The mother feels sad and grieves over lost expectations. Disillusionment continues and builds into depression. A feeling of hopelessness sets in. She senses she has lost control of her life. She blames herself and everyone and everything around her — her children, spouse or significant partner, her work and co-workers.

Her health problems intensify. This "dis-ease" phase can include migraine headaches, ulcers, irritable bowel syndrome, among other problems. Her fatigue becomes chronic. She visits her physician more often, receiving more and more prescriptions for depression, anxiety or sleep disorders. Substance abuse is common. Her use of alcohol, smoking or caffeine accelerates. All of these compound the depression.

STAGE 4. DETACHMENT

Detachment from others occurs. This results from a feeling of being overwhelmed and from a lack of energy. Apathy, cynicism, mistrust and paranoia fuel this part of the process. She withdraws emotionally from family and friends. Her daily chores become drudgery. Family demands are too overwhelming and fatigue intensifies. She feels an urgent need to get away from everybody, but anger and resentment make her feel trapped.

STAGE 5. DYSFUNCTION

Dysfunction impacts the mother mentally, emotionally and physically. In this final stage every aspect of her life is touched. She may become completely debilitated. Fatigue becomes exhaustion, a state that immobilizes her. Daily tasks cannot be completed. It is difficult for her to care for herself or for her family.

Professional help is essential in the later stages. Physicians, psychologists, psychotherapists, family counselors, social workers and clergy offer a supportive team approach. Recovery from stages 4 and 5 is slow and may take many months or years. The devastating effects of burnout on mothers and their families are grossly underestimated.

On a positive note, you can prevent burnout or pull yourself out of the process in the first three stages. Awareness is crucial. Once the signals of possible burnout are understood, you can apply immediate stress management strategies. Deep breathing, relaxation tapes, warm baths and venting with a friend are all helpful. But they are not enough. You must assert yourself. You need to say no to some demands, refuse new commitments and resign current involvements. You must reduce your workload and let go of some tasks.

To replenish your depleted energy resources, increase the time you allow for sleep and take frequent breaks throughout the day. Try to get away for a day and pamper yourself. Eat more nutritiously, exercise, play with the children. Pull on your sense of humor and laugh more.

Identify your present energy level. Check one.

□ Exhausted □ Fatigued □ Low Energy
□ Moderate Energy □ High Energy

If you checked any of the first three, re-read the last three paragraphs.

List one action step you can take *now* to prevent burnout or to begin pulling out.

_____

When are you going to start?

_____

How many minutes per day are you willing to take to re-energize yourself?

_____

What is your health and function worth to you?

_____

_____

Act Now — Make Choices

You can take control of your life in three simple steps:

1. Identify and analyze your stressors (causes of stress).
2. Work each stressor through a problem-solving process.
3. Learn coping concepts that enable immediate stress relief.

IDENTIFY YOUR STRESSORS

Do you know what is causing your stress? Have you listed the people or situations that produce pressure? This exercise yields instant relief. When your mind is stressed and too overwhelmed to function, unload it by writing things down. You can't take care of your stress if you haven't identified the cause.

You need to remember that stressors can be internal or external. Worry, depression, anxiety and guilt are examples of internal stress. You can include others such as substance abuse, injury, illness and hormonal fluctuations. Premenstrual syndrome (PMS), pregnancy or menopause can also induce stress.

External sources of stress include noise, inadequate lighting, temperature, atmospheric changes, contaminated air or water and exposure to chemicals. Financial crises, unemployment and family problems are other examples.

Major life events (a death in the family) and daily hassles (lost car keys) produce stress and impact your health and energy levels. Significant losses require mothers and families to work through a grieving process, which can be draining. Research has found that the potential for illness increases as the number of major life changes increases over a given period of time.

Stressors can have both positive and negative effects. For instance, a new job would be challenging and exciting, yet it could bring new pressures. A new addition to the family could be positive, yet bring stressful family adjustments. Your body reacts the same way whether a stressor is positive or negative. The difference is that the body's stress response resolves faster with positive stressors.

Take this self-test to help your thinking. Check those items below that have been producing stress in your life during the past 12 months.

_____ Conflicts in marriage or in significant relationships

_____ Marital separation

_____ Divorce

_____ Single parent

_____ Stepparent

_____ Constant worrying about the children

_____ Move to a new home

_____ Financial crisis

_____ Car/transportation problems

_____ Inability to balance roles

_____ Back to school

_____ No time for me

_____ Your illness/injury/surgery

_____ Illness of child

_____ Behavior problems of a child

_____ Sibling rivalry

_____ Child refuses to do chores

_____ Adolescent challenges

_____ Communication break-
down in the family

_____ Addition or loss of family
member

_____ Can't meet the demands
of relatives

_____ Increase in neighborhood
crime

_____ Overinvolvement in
community

_____ No social life

These are general stressors. Now, try to be more specific. For example, "Kevin has daily stomachaches and doesn't want to go to school." Being clear hastens the problem-solving process.

Add your specific stressors.

_____

_____

_____

_____

Write one specific stressor in your personal life.

_____

_____

You need to include stressors from all aspects of your life, your work life too. Do you find yourself in conflict with your supervisor? Is there stress within co-worker relationships? Are you unable to adapt to constant change? Is your work environment causing any stress? Are your present roles and tasks positive?

List three work stressors.

_____

_____

_____

Write one specific stressor in your work life.

_____

_____

Now, you need to differentiate between stressors. Go back to the checklist and your additions. Next to each, place an "I" if the stressor is infrequent or a "C" if it is chronic. Occasional stressors are not a problem because you are resilient and bounce back.

Your _chronic stressors_ are the problem. Constant stress dumps hormones into your bloodstream that impact all body systems. They keep you hyper-alert and drain you of energy. Over time this damages your health.

PROBLEM-SOLVE YOUR STRESSORS

Now that you have identified your stressors, your next task is to resolve the sources of prolonged stress. Take each stressor through a problem-solving process by means of the four little letters that can change your life: ECAC. They stand for _eliminate, change, accept_ and _cope._

Write down one of your specific chronic stressors.

_____

_____

_____

Ask yourself these four questions:

1. Can I Eliminate This Stressor?

If the answer is yes, state how you might remove it from your life.

_____

_____

If the answer is no, go to step 2. Some stressors cannot be eliminated.

2. Can I Change This Situation To Reduce My Stress?

You can call on your creative abilities during this part of the process. List how you might modify this situation to make things tolerable. For instance, you can change your attitude toward someone or something. You can alter the way you perceive events. Most important, you have the power to change the way you respond to a stressor. You can intercept your conditioned response and react differently. This takes practice. I'm not saying it's easy, but it can be done.

List one step you can take to alter the situation to reduce the stress.

_____

_____

3. Can I Accept What I Cannot Change?

You might find this difficult if you tend to be too controlling. If you resist accepting what you cannot control and change, you risk self-destruction.

Acceptance involves letting go and is essential to your survival. You can waste tremendous energy fighting things that are beyond your control. Save that energy.

Ask yourself if this stressor is in your control. Can you do something about it? If you can't, choose to accept it and then let it go. This can free up your energy. Your energy should be directed toward things you can control and do something about. Some mothers reduce their stress by half with this decision.

Acceptance is not apathy, so don't confuse the two. You decide to let go after analyzing the stressor. You can decide to release rather than to resist. This is powerful. It can save your health and even your life.

Are you ready to work on acceptance and letting go?

_____ Yes _____ No

Write one stressor that you might decide to accept in order to cope.

_____

_____

4. Can I Use Coping Skills?

Coping means choosing to act rather than react. It means taking a proactive stance when faced with a stressful situation. You can make it simple, such as taking a deep breath, laughing, repeating an affirmation or adjusting an attitude. You can practice skills that take time to develop, such as meditation, imagery or muscle tensing and relaxing. Learn as many strategies as you can.

Write one coping skill you could practice.

_____

_____

_____

COPING CONCEPTS

As the only person in charge of your life, the only one who can change it, you need to remember these coping concepts:

1. To an extent, stress is a matter of perception.
2. A sense of control buffers the stress response.

Stress starts in the mind. It is your perception of the stressor, not the stressor itself, that determines the body's response. As you evaluate each situation, your mind decides if, when and how intensely you are going to react. The mind dictates to the body, and the body communicates back to the mind. This mind/body feedback system is continuous and cannot be separated.

This is an empowering concept. It means you can engineer your reaction to stress by changing how you view a person or event. Sometimes you condition yourself to respond in a certain way to a specific stressor. This automatic response can be intercepted by altering the mind. Try it. You can start perceiving some stressors as opportunities rather than as threats. When you start seeing them as challenges, your stress levels will plummet.

Are you willing to change your perception of one person or situation to reduce your stress?

_____ Yes _____ No

Who or what would it be?

_____

_____

The second concept is equally important. Mothers who believe they have little control over their lives have higher stress levels. These women are called "external locus of control" people. They do not believe that they have choices in life. Consequently they blame other people for their choices and life outcomes.

"Internal locus of control" mothers believe they have choices. They sense control over life's challenges. They accept responsibility for the decisions they make. These women take charge of their stress levels, rather than allowing stress to immobilize them. Their stress levels are lower.

Are you an external or an internal locus of control mother?

_____

_____

_____

If you are an external person, you can convert this negative trait by changing your attitude, belief system and perception of life events.

Take charge of your life — not tomorrow, not next week, but *now*. Your health, energy and ability to function are keys to your family's survival. You can learn to manage the stress in your life.

Model For Health And Energy

Use moderate stress to motivate you and yield top performance

Listen to your stress signals to start coping: ■ Change perceptions/ reactions ■ Use coping skills

Prevent burnout through awareness of the burnout process

Pull out of burnout: ■ Cut workload ■ Use stress management ■ Replenish energy stores ■ Seek professional help

Identify and analyze your stressors

Problem-solve stressors: ■ Eliminate them ■ Change perception/ reaction ■ Accept what cannot be changed ■ Cope better

Be an internal locus of control person: ■ Believe you have choices ■ Accept responsibility for yourself

Take charge of your life *today* to yield health and energy.

2

Who's Pushing Your Buttons?

I release my guilt, anger and self-destructive behaviors

Push. React. Push. React. Are your buttons being pushed all day long? Do you respond automatically, feeling manipulated? Do you know who or what makes you react? Are you frustrated and angry because you're out of control?

Your emotional and behavioral reactions evolved over a lifetime. They didn't pop up yesterday or the day before. Your personality, programming, genetic makeup, biochemical differences and learned behaviors all played a part. Conditioning takes time.

Some personality traits and behaviors can be self-defeating, jeopardizing your health and energy as a mother. Patterns you may not even recognize as self-destructive can cause three major problems:

- They drain away your time and energy.
- They escalate your stress level, causing conflicts in your relationships.
- They model unhealthy behaviors for your children, who are vulnerable to adapting them.

Button One: Perfectionism

Many mothers strive for perfection despite the fact that no one can be perfect. The illusion of perfection seduces mothers and promotes an excessive drive to push toward unrealistic goals . . . achievements that cannot be humanly attained. This brings chronic disappointment, frustration and unhappiness, and self-esteem plummets.

Are you a perfectionist? Check those that apply to you.

_____ Do you feel you need to be perfect to gain approval from others?

_____ Do you procrastinate about projects until you can do them "just right"?

_____ Are you frustrated at home and at work because no one understands your need to have things perfect?

_____ Are you convinced you can do everything perfectly if only you try harder?

_____ Do you rationalize your perfectionism by telling yourself you are setting a good example for the children?

_____ Do you believe you will achieve happiness by being a perfectionist?

_____ Are you exhausted, but keep trying to have things perfect?

_____ Is your behavior compulsive? Are you compelled to do a task because it must be done now?

If you checked four or more, you may be a perfectionist. Examine your behavior. Assess to what degree it might be a problem with home and work relationships. How is this behavior affecting your health and energy levels?

Compulsive

How compulsive are you? Do you rush to empty a wastepaper basket when someone puts one dirty tissue in it? Are you frustrated when things are not in their place? Are you unable to go to bed at night until your sink is empty and your kitchen is spotless? If you answer yes to these, you may have a problem.

Perfectionists are driven by the irrational belief that life, work and family can be perfect if they try hard enough. The ramifications of this striving are serious. A continuous outpouring of energy drains these mothers.

People Pleasers

Perfectionists are often pleasers. In addition to doing things "just right," they strive to please everyone. They rationalize this behavior by assuring themselves that giving, giving, giving brings acceptance and approval from others.

Fearful

Limitations go unrecognized by perfectionists. These mothers do not allow themselves to be human, to make mistakes or to do less than what they feel they must do. They may have strong fears of rejection and failure. Stressful behavior evolves from these fears.

Procrastinators

Many perfectionists are procrastinators. Frozen by the fear of failure, or sometimes the fear of success, they delay top priority tasks.

They might delay starting for fear of not doing a project just right. They may keep doing an assignment over and over until it is perfect. Often, they wait for the right time to do the job right. Invariably they complete tasks just under-the-wire or late. They rationalize this behavior by saying they work better under pressure.

Procrastination triggers anxiety and chronic stress. This stress overload is a problem at home and at work. Perfectionists can be a handicap in the workplace. Co-worker conflicts may arise because of their procrastination.

This problem is exacerbated where teamwork is vital. As perfectionists delay doing their part of a project, they hold other team members up. Missed deadlines create havoc not only for the business, but for the clients. The repercussions are great. Perfectionists can be a liability as stress-carriers.

Unrealistic Standards

Needing to do a perfect job and wanting to do a good job are different. With perfectionism you have excessive and unrealistic standards. In working toward excellence and doing a good job, you have high standards, but they are realistic.

Perfectionist Children

Think about your children. Children imitate behaviors. Do you see any evidence of perfectionist traits in them? Do they burst into tears if they can't print or write their assignment just right? Are they frustrated and angry or put themselves down if they don't win in a sports event? Are they sad or depressed when they don't get perfect scores on all their tests?

Energy Drain

Imagine the energy drain from perfectionism. Visualize the never-ending energy output for an illusion . . . something that doesn't exist . . . something that can never be. Understand how this chronic drain affects your health and causes fatigue. Imagine the strain on relationships. Recognize that such behavior is self-destructive. Determine if this perfect illusion is worth it.

There are many ways to overcome self-defeating behaviors. Professional help is essential, particularly if your perfectionism is compulsive.

Are you a perfectionist?
_____ Yes _____ No

To what degree is perfectionism a problem?

_____

_____

Are your children showing signs of perfectionism?
_____ Yes _____ No

Button Two:
Type A Makes A Superwoman

Most mothers are a blend of Type A (hurried) and Type B (laid back), but some are predominantly Type A. They have many positive qualities; however, in terms of energy drain, fatigue and health, extreme Type A mothers may have problems.

To what degree are you Type A? Read each question carefully, then write in the appropriate number using the following key:

1. Never
2. Sometimes
3. Frequently
4. Constantly

_____ Do you eat fast, stand while eating or constantly get up and down from the table?

_____ Are you continuously telling your children to hurry?

_____ Do you feel a satisfying "rush" when gunning your car through a yellow light or speeding around a slow driver?

_____ Do you explode when your child causes a minor accident (knocks a plastic item off a shelf or spills a beverage)?

_____ Are you aggressive when someone cuts in front of you?

_____ Do you watch every penny while checking groceries out because you believe the clerk will cheat you?

_____ When unexpected events occur, are you frustrated because of the time pressures you feel?

_____ Are you enraged when waiting in line behind an older person who needs help?

_____ Do you brag to your friends about how many projects you can complete in a day?

_____ Is it impossible for you to relax in the evening because you feel the pressure of unfinished tasks?

Scoring: If you scored 20 or less, you are doing fine. If you scored 21-30, take a good look at your behavior as it relates to health, function and relationships. If you scored 31-40, your behavior may be interfering with your work and family life.

Type A behavior has been redefined over the past 30 years. Today the identified qualities for Type A individuals do not always cause health risks.

Four traits of extreme Type A mothers are significant:

• Time urgency
• Competitiveness
• Need to control
• Anger, rage and hostility

TIME URGENCY

Type A mothers sense a *time urgency.* They become obsessed with time and squeeze more and more tasks into smaller and smaller amounts of time. They constantly measure their performance against the clock to check if they are reaching their self-imposed deadlines.

COMPETITIVENESS

Type A women are highly *competitive*

and strive to be superwomen. They believe they can have it all without paying a price. Juggling more and more tasks becomes a competitive challenge. They believe they can give 150 percent to their increased activities 100 percent of the time. Energy becomes a problem.

NUMBERS GAME

Numbers fascinate them. They become intrigued with how many of what can be pumped out by what time. They pride themselves on how many things they can achieve in a day or can cross off their to-do list.

Polyphasic Behavior

They develop a polyphasic behavior pattern (doing three and four things at once). Every mother does several things at once at times, but with Type A women, this behavior is chronic.

The time urgency, competitiveness and numbers game result in hurried or busy behavior that can become compulsive. Their pace increases. They walk fast, eat fast and talk fast, which drains their energy. Since their minds are also on fast speed, their relationships are marked by communication problems.

LISTENING PROBLEMS

Extreme Type A mothers have difficulty *listening*. They cannot slow down to hear what other people say. While someone is talking, they are formulating a response in their minds.

They interrupt their children and adults in conversations. They finish sentences for others because of their impatience and the time urgency that they feel. Slow and relaxed conversations are intolerable.

Mental Racing

This mental racing creates other problems. Driven by urgency and time pressures, they don't relax before bedtime, so they awaken at night, can't fall back to sleep and experience extreme anxiety. These mothers spend the night counting the remaining hours before they need to jump on their treadmill again.

NEED TO CONTROL

Extreme Type A mothers sense a *need to control* their environment. This need to manage people and situations is intense and includes both their home and work lives. Failure to control their surroundings brings great frustration.

These mothers are great organizers. They often volunteer to take charge of activities because this fulfills their need to be in control. However, they often overcommit and overextend themselves. Driven by this inner demand, their energy reserves drain away.

ANGER, RAGE, HOSTILITY

Anger, rage and hostility are toxic and the most damaging of the Type A qualities. They are fueled by the competitiveness, hurried behavior, cynical attitude and mistrust that extreme Type A mothers exhibit. Prolonged anger and hostility can put mothers at risk for heart disease and other health problems.

Biochemical Factors

What drives Type A women? Probably several factors. First, there can be biochemical factors. Most significant is a higher level of norepinephrine (noradrenaline), which probably fuels the hurrying about. Cholesterol and triglycerides (fatty substances in the bloodstream) can also be elevated. Chronic elevated levels are not healthy. Heredity and life experiences may also be important factors.

Learned Behavior

Type A behavior can be learned. Over time, women who are more laid back (Type B) can develop Type A qualities and behaviors after, for example, working in a fast-lane environment that promotes competitiveness and urgent deadlines.

Corporate America rewards excessive Type A behavior and workaholism. Promotions often go to women who are ambitious go-getters, and who are competitive, enthusiastic and thrive on speed.

Conflicts arise when these women fail to appreciate the different personalities within their departments. Type A supervisors may be intolerant of more relaxed employees. These slower paced women may be equally efficient, but they are not always valued in today's workplace.

Are you a Type A mother?

_____ Yes _____ No

If yes, do you feel that your health, energy levels or relationships are in jeopardy?

_____ Yes _____ No

Would you like to modify your behavior?

_____ Yes _____ No

It is the extreme behavior you want to look at, the extreme behavior that becomes self-destructive.

6 Tips For Changing Self-Destructive Behaviors

Both perfectionism and Type A behavior can be modified with help and support.

1. BECOME AWARE

Begin by tuning into your behavior and emotions. Log your observations in a journal and examine your behavioral patterns. Determine the extent to which your behavior threatens your health, energy levels and relationships.

Get in touch with the "why" of your behavior. What makes you strive so? Is it for approval? Is it for acceptance? Do you have to prove yourself? Are you compulsive? How severely are you driven?

Read books on perfectionism or Type A behavior to increase your awareness. Take a class in changing behavior patterns at a community college or adult education program. Make a commitment, admit you have a problem and take responsibility to change. Pull on your support system.

2. GET PROFESSIONAL HELP

This is necessary if your behavior falls in the extreme, particularly if your perfectionist or "hurried" behavior has become compulsive.

3. EXAMINE PERSONAL AND PROFESSIONAL EXPECTATIONS

Determine whether your goals and standards for yourself and others are realistic. See if your standards need to be lowered.

Let go of your need to have everyone's approval; it cannot happen. Understand that you do not have to constantly prove yourself. Accept the fact that everyone has limitations. Learn to say no without guilt, build your self-esteem and become assertive. Start ridding yourself of excess commitments.

4. START SMALL

Change comes very slow. Choose one behavioral change at a time. For instance, with perfectionism, if you are compulsively vacuuming every night, you might choose to vacuum five nights a week or every other night. Over time, reduce the activity. You might deliberately choose to leave the dishes in the sink overnight. This is very hard to do, but you can do it.

You might need to work on procrastination. Break down large projects into small tasks, reward yourself for not procrastinating and take small risks in order to work through your fears.

Make minor changes to slow down, such as chewing each mouthful 20 times before swallowing and taking the next bite.

You might decide that every time you feel impatient, you will take a deep breath. Every time you catch yourself gunning your car through a yellow light, you might drive around the block and approach the traffic light again.

Focus on one thought at a time. Do one task at a time and complete it. Don't wear your watch on weekends. Try to enjoy the moment, rediscover your sense of humor, become more flexible and appreciate each family member more. Be a better listener. Over time, these changes will slow your behavior.

By slowing down your actions, you will expend less energy and feel more energetic. Pamper and nurture yourself to restore your energy reserve. As you become less rigid, your relationships will improve, your stress will lessen, and you will gradually come to feel in charge of your life.

5. COACH YOURSELF

The way you talk to yourself makes a big difference. Instead of listening to that critical inner voice year after year, begin to modify your inner dialogue. To counteract perfectionism, give yourself permission to do a good job. Speak kindly and tell yourself that it is fine to strive for excellence, but not okay to strive for an illusion-like perfectionism. Ease up on family members too when they are doing the best they can.

With extreme Type A behavior, tell yourself it's okay not to be a superwoman. Reinforce the idea that you can slow down and be just as efficient. Speed doesn't make a better mother or a better worker. Share with your family that you are trying to change.

You need their unconditional support.

6. ALLOW YOURSELF TO BE HUMAN

During any change, setbacks occur. The old destructive behaviors creep in when you are most vulnerable. Be kind to yourself if this happens. Allow a margin for error. Then, continue changing, knowing that you will be healthier, have more energy and improve your relationships.

Write one action step you can take to work on perfectionism or extreme Type A behavior.

Button Three: Guilt

This is the guilty generation. Mothers feel guilty if they stay at home and guilty if they work outside the home. They feel guilty if they do too much for their children, guilty if they don't do enough for their children. There is no letup. Guilt is a pervasive emotion that can drain off precious energy.

Some single mothers suffer tremendous guilt because they are particularly hard on themselves. They feel guilty for not being able to give their children what they want. They regret not being able to live at a certain standard of living. They suffer pangs of inadequacy. Irrationally, they feel guilty for not being able to be two

people. None of these reasons deserves guilt, yet this emotion is intense.

Is guilt all bad? No. Some guilt is positive. It can even become the guardian of your behavior. It can prevent you from making serious mistakes.

Guilt can also motivate, providing energy needed for action. If you've made a mistake and you feel guilty, this remorse can move you to take action.

Guilt facilitates learning from a past event. It becomes a tool for a proactive stance. To that extent, guilt can be helpful. Guilt can be constructive and help you achieve goals. Brief guilt, acted upon, is not a problem.

Guilt becomes a problem when it is prolonged and excessive. Ongoing guilt brings serious consequences. Study the guilt cycle. (See Figure 2.1)

As guilt persists, it *paralyzes* you, affecting both your mind and body. Your mind distorts events, and your thoughts become irrational. The longer you live with guilt, the worse this becomes. Your ability to stand up for yourself weakens. Your effort to adapt to this lethargy drains you of energy resources, and you become an easy target for *manipulation*.

Manipulation

Your children know exactly when you are down and can't say no. From birth, they are brilliant manipulators, and their talents increase as they grow older. By adolescence they are pros. They become experts in when and how to push your buttons. You become putty in their hands.

Overcompensation

Overcompensation results from your excessive guilt and the children's

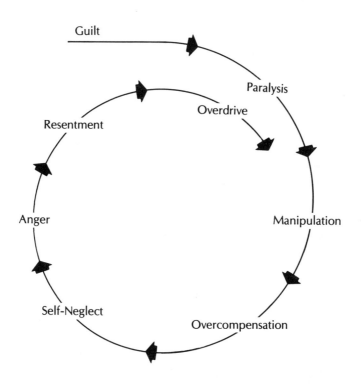

Figure 2.1. The Guilt Cycle

manipulation. You give in to your children's requests and do more and more for them, which has tremendous repercussions on your finances and energy levels.

The more money you spend on your children, often beyond your means, the more guilty you become. You believe that buying things will take care of their manipulation and your guilt, but it only worsens the situation.

This cycle must stop for everyone's sake. It's time to say no.

Overcompensation hurts you in another way. It robs your energy resources, causing fatigue. You rush around at the children's slightest whim. You drive them to the mall or to extracurricular activities. You run them over to a friend's house, without their chores being done. You take charge of their school assignments. Guilt is a potent driver.

Self-Neglect

Self-neglect results from overcompensation. Mothers who feel tremendous guilt put everyone else's needs above their own. Despite their depleted energy reserves, they put out, put out, put out. Unfortunately, they stop nurturing themselves.

Anger

Anger results when giving, giving, giving catches up with you. Your frustration gives way to *resentment* toward those nearest and dearest to you. Family relationships are strained and in jeopardy.

Overdrive

Overdrive sets in because you are feeling guilty over these family conflicts. You drive harder, deplete more energy and the vicious guilt cycle starts once again.

Let Go Of Feeling Guilty

Would you give anything to stop feeling guilty? Do you want to break the cycle that has you immobilized? Remember, deep-seated guilt and prolonged remorse probably require professional help. Therapy and support are necessary for repressed guilt from earlier traumatic events that still affect you. However, current guilt can be dealt with in many ways:

1. ADMIT THAT YOU HAVE A PROBLEM WITH GUILT

Resolve to work on it. Recognize that you are one person, and give yourself time to change this self-defeating pattern.

2. JUSTIFY YOUR GUILT

Intercept your guilty feelings early on. Write down the reason why you feel guilty. Explore the situation that made you feel guilty.

Ask yourself:

What is the current reason for feeling guilty?

Is there a valid reason for your guilt?

Write down three ways in which your feeling guilty can change this situation.

Write down three problems that can result from your preoccupation with guilt.

Is feeling guilty going to help you in this situation?

If you answered yes, write how.

3. MAKE GUILT WORK FOR YOU

Channel your guilt in a positive way. Say: "I refuse to feel guilty. I don't deserve this." Sit down and problem-solve immediately. Act. If you made a mistake, confirm it, set it right, then let it go. If you unintentionally hurt someone, apologize, make amends, then release the guilt. Refuse to carry the guilt into future events.

4. HOLD A CONFERENCE WITH YOUR CHILDREN

Before you confer with your children, identify for yourself what you want to be different within your family dynamics. Inform your children that manipulation will no longer be tolerated. Communicate that there will be some changes. For example, requests for chauffering will not be honored unless household chore assignments have been completed. Be firm. Hold your ground. Listen to their feedback.

5. STOP YOUR MIND FROM DWELLING ON GUILT

You can divert yourself in many ways: listen to music, read, write, watch television or do handicrafts or household activities.

List one step you can take to work with your guilt if it is a problem.

_____

_____

Button Four: Anger — The Domino Effect

Anger is a normal emotion experienced by most people. Some anger is justified. For example, you make a dinner date with a good friend to share exciting news about your new job. You arrive at the restaurant a few minutes early. Your friend never shows up. This disappointment can spark some valid anger. Deal with this feeling as soon as possible.

Perhaps there was a good reason why she didn't come. Maybe she was in a minor automobile accident after work and in the confusion forgot about dinner, or maybe she had an overwhelmingly stressful day and didn't check her calendar before leaving for home. Stress causes these problems.

Call her immediately. Using "I" statements, tell her how disappointed you are and ask her what happened. Give her time to explain because she will probably be devastated at having forgotten your date. Resolve the anger right then and there.

Conditioning And Rage

Some mothers, instead of dealing with their anger, suppress it. It simmers away. Many women have difficulty in dealing with anger in part because of society's conditioning, which tells young girls, "Be nice. Don't ruffle any feathers. Don't cause conflicts. Don't fight."

Simmering anger leads to rage, which touches everyone and everything. Its domino effect ripples through the entire family, straining and destroying relationships. This suppressed emotion presents itself in explosive behavior, in overreacting to minor events and in verbal abuse. Victims are affected mentally and emotionally, and sometimes physical abuse occurs. Anger at home accompanies the mother to the workplace, again causing the domino effect.

Chronic Anger

Chronic anger destroys a mother's health. Adrenaline fuels the anger, which not only taxes the adrenal glands, but also drains energy. Remember, chronic anger, rage and hostility are toxic.

Mothers who scream at their children convey certain messages:

"I am out of control."

"I can be manipulated."

Most mothers do not like feeling out of control. When you explode or overreact, you give control of your life over to your children. You lose power . . . your children gain power.

Are you a reactor?

_____ Yes _____ No

Do you have a child who pushes your buttons easily?

_____ Yes _____ No

Do you feel manipulated?

_____ Yes _____ No

Is your anger too frequent?

_____ Yes _____ No

Is your anger too intense?

_____ Yes _____ No

Is your anger out of control?

_____ Yes _____ No

---

5 Ways To Intercept Manipulation And Anger

1. LOG YOUR BEHAVIOR

Watch your reactions for two weeks. Keep a journal in which you write down angry situations, who manipulates you, how you behave, your level of control, your feelings and insights. Look for repeated patterns.

2. RECOGNIZE ONCOMING MANIPULATION AND ANGER

Make a decision. Substitute another action. Deep breathe immediately and count up to 30 or use positive phrasing, such as, "I am in control. I refuse to be manipulated." Call a time out. Cool down and get back in control. Then you can address the issue more objectively.

3. DON'T FUEL YOUR ANGER

When adrenaline is flooding your body, avoid using substances that trigger the stress response and increase already high adrenaline levels, such as caffeine, nicotine and alcohol.

4. EVALUATE YOUR RELATIONSHIPS

Decide to let go of some of the manipulative relationships in your life. Of course, you can't do that with your immediate family, but you can make such decisions about friends and relatives who trigger chronic destructive behavior. Even at work you can decide to avoid or limit your interactions with certain individuals who are unhealthy for you. Surround yourself with positive people.

5. IDENTIFY CONSTRUCTIVE ACTIONS

Exercise, cleaning and physical activities of any kind help dissipate the stress chemicals. Writing a letter to the person you are angry with is helpful. Hold back the letter for three or four days to decide if you are going to send it or burn it. Visualize the manipulator sitting across from you and vent your anger. Use music, relaxation tapes or vent the anger with your best friend. Take an anger awareness class. Get professional help if necessary.

Some mothers feel that their children have no right to feel angry. This isn't true. Your children have a right to express feelings. Acknowledge their feelings and provide them with healthy outlets for their anger, too.

Model For Health And Energy

Look at your perfectionism or Type A behavior that: ■ Drains time and energy ■ Escalates stress ■ Models unhealthy behavior	Study the guilt cycle: ■ Paralysis, manipulation, overcompensation, self-neglect, anger, resentment and overdrive	Modify behavior: ■ Increase awareness and get professional help ■ Start small changes ■ Coach yourself and allow temporary setbacks
Be aware of: ■ Perfectionism — the elusive drive toward unrealistic goals ■ Extreme Type A qualities like: 1. Time urgency 2. Competitiveness 3. Need for control 4. Anger and hostility	Break the guilt cycle: ■ Admit a problem and justify your guilt ■ Make guilt work for you — problem-solve and act ■ Hold a family conference and stop manipulation	Intercept anger and manipulation: ■ Substitute an activity for the anger ■ Limit caffeine, nicotine and alcohol ■ Eliminate manipulative relationships ■ Identify healthy outlets for anger
		Release guilt, anger and self-destructive behavior to yield health and energy.

3

Breathe —
It's A Life-Giving Skill

*I breathe deeply
for energy*

If you were offered a coping skill that used no equipment and cost nothing, would you use it? Would you welcome a technique that energizes as well as relaxes?

Breathing correctly is a potent force that has a positive impact on your mind and body. It determines your energy level and can make or break your pool of energy. Learning breathing techniques may be one of the most important choices of a lifetime.

Stop for a minute right now. Focus on your chest and abdomen. Is either moving as you breathe quietly? Is your breathing so shallow your chest isn't moving? Or are you breathing deeply, allowing your abdomen to move rhythmically with every inhalation and exhalation?

Answer these questions:

1. My chest and abdomen do not move when I breathe.
_____ True _____ False

2. My chest goes out, then in, as I breathe.
_____ True _____ False

3. My abdomen rises, then falls as I breathe.
_____ True _____ False

27

If you answered true to number one, you could be a very tired mother. You are denying yourself a dynamic pool of energy by breathing incorrectly. This is particularly true if this is your regular pattern of breathing.

If you answered true to number two, you are a chest breather. You are not taking advantage of all the energy you could have.

If you answered true to number three, congratulations. You are using your energy potential by breathing abdominally.

Pause again. Check your posture right now. How are you sitting?

I am slouching. My shoulders are down. My chest and abdomen are squeezed together.
_____ True _____ False

I am sitting upright. My shoulders are up and slightly back. My chest and abdomen are free to move with my breathing.
_____ True _____ False

If you answered true to the first question, you are immobilizing your lungs — your life-giving organs. You are preventing energy from reaching you. A true response to number two means that your lungs are free to work for you. The breathing techniques discussed in this chapter can change your life and energy level.

The Big Deal About Breathing

Incredible as it sounds, many mothers use only a portion of their lungs. If you use only half of your lungs, you are depriving yourself of vital energy. Minimal air taken in during inhalation means decreased oxygen, and less oxygen means less energy. This may be one reason why mothers are so tired.

Emptying your lungs only partially can be a problem. The lungs filter out air pollutants. Carbon dioxide (CO_2) and other toxins are released when you exhale. If you exhale only a fraction of these gases, the lungs still have most of the stagnant air, carbon dioxide and toxins. This prevents fresh air from being taken in. Study the diagram of the lung of a shallow breather versus an abdominal breather. (See Figure 3.1)

Look at the amount of fresh air (with oxygen) taken in, then check the different levels of stagnant air, carbon dioxide and toxins remaining in the lungs. Look at the different energy levels. You have two lungs, so either double the loss (shallow breather) or double the gain (abdominal breather). Which are you?

You Can Have Much More

Every minute of your life you are breathing. In just one minute, while you are reading this page, you will breathe 12-16 times. In one hour you will breathe approximately 840 times. Think of the potential you have to engineer your energy through good breathing techniques.

Within your lungs, a miracle occurs every day of your life. Oxygen and other gases are pulled into your lungs when you inhale fresh air. The oxygen is picked up by tiny blood vessels.

Hemoglobin, a substance within your red blood cells, is the transport system in the bloodstream that car-

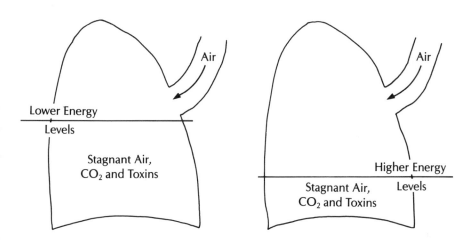

Figure 3.1. Shallow Breather Versus Abdominal Breather

ries the oxygen throughout your body. The brain and muscles are major recipients.

Mothers who smoke sabotage this transport system. The carbon monoxide from smoking clings to the hemoglobin and displaces the oxygen. Mothers who smoke are tired from reduced oxygen.

Oxygen = Energy

Oxygen is crucial for human functioning. Your brain cannot operate without it. Thinking and speaking depend on this necessary substance.

Your body also requires oxygen to fuel its functioning. At home, on the job or at school, there is a continuous demand for oxygen.

Athletes and entertainers give us good examples of conscious breathing. Singers and stage performers use controlled breathing as part of their pre-performance warm-up. Basketball players take a deep breath prior to a free throw. Olympic swimming competitors consciously gulp air for oxygen immediately before the gun.

Assess Your Breathing

How can you tell if your breathing is abdominal? While standing, place a hand right above your belly button. While inhaling, if your hand moves out, it is a deep breath. Another test is to lie down with a light book right above the navel. If the book rises with inhalation and falls with exhalation, your diaphragm is at work.

Monitor your breathing for one week. Check yourself on the hour every two hours as a reminder (7:00, 9:00, 11:00 and so forth). Try to "catch yourself" breathing. Document your observations.

1. What is your breathing rhythm? Is it smooth or erratic? Is it fast? Is it slow?
2. Is your breathing shallow? Is there no movement of your chest or abdomen? Or are you breathing deeply?
3. Scan your chest muscles. Are you experiencing tightness within your chest? Or are your chest muscles fully relaxed?
4. What is your level of stress right now? High, moderate or low?

After you have evaluated your breathing patterns for one week, make some general statements.

My breathing rhythm has been

_____.

I have been a shallow breather _____ part of the time, _____ most of the time _____ or all of the time. Generally speaking, my level of stress has been _____.

You may find that the greater the stress, the faster you're breathing. This is part of the stress response. But fast breathing can cause you to hyperventilate, which occurs when too much carbon dioxide is released. This upset in your critical balance of oxygen and carbon dioxide can cause you to feel light-headed or mentally fuzzy.

You might find that during times of high stress you feel a tightness in your chest. Your chest muscles are powerful, and under stress they constrict, squeezing your lungs. This prevents the lungs from fully expanding and shallow breathing results. You might even be holding your breath, which means that less and less air can reach your lungs. Tiredness is due to your reduced supply of oxygen.

What have you observed about your breathing pattern?

Breathing Works

What do mothers say about their breathing exercises? Conscious breathing:

"Clears my head."
"Helps me gain control."
"Relaxes me so I can sleep."
"Slows down my racing mind."
"Releases my physical tension."

Women who have developed a good breathing habit can eventually measure its physiological effects. If you want to try it yourself, first take your pulse rate before doing the breathing exercises. Then, after three to five minutes, retake your pulse. You may well find that your pulse rate decreases. "It's a natural tranquilizer." Are you ready to try it?

Breathe — It's As Easy As 1-2-3

THE CALMING BREATH

Sit up straight. Uncross your knees. Loosen any tight clothing. Place your hands on your thighs.

1. With your mouth closed, *inhale* through your nostrils as deeply as you can for 3-4 seconds. Draw in the fresh air to your abdomen. Make your diaphragm work for you.

2. *Hold* the breath 3-4 seconds.
3. *Exhale* by puckering your lips, then *SLOWLY* blow the breath out through your mouth, about 5-6 seconds. The slow exhalation helps to empty stagnant air and carbon dioxide out of the lungs. The lungs are never completely emptied.

Breathe normally now. Follow each calming breath with regular breathing. Take 4-5 regular breaths between each deep breath. Several stress experts suggest a series of three abdominal breaths separated by normal breathing. This is powerful. This full exercise takes about 1½ minutes.

How did the deep breath feel?

_____

_____.

Breathe with ease. Never force a breath. Some mothers try too hard. They force the whole breath, upsetting the delicate balance of oxygen and carbon dioxide, and they get dizzy. If this happens to you, stop. Next time you take a deep breath, don't breathe so deeply. Go slow, go easy. Don't work at it. Just let it happen.

Breathing exercises take practice and commitment. But they are worth it. Eventually, you can extend your length of inhaling, holding and exhaling. For example, after weeks or months of regular exercise, the blowing out can be extended to 6-8 seconds.

ABDOMINAL BREATHING

Why is it so important to breathe abdominally? The diaphragm is a sheet of muscle that separates the chest from the abdomen. When you inhale, the muscle goes downward to allow full lung expansion. When you exhale, it rises to help you empty out the toxins.

Abdominal breathing allows the greatest intake of air. If you were ever a brass player, wind player or singer, you were instructed to use abdominal breathing. Your performance depended on it.

During pregnancy, you may have learned breathing exercises. Through Lamaze Childbirth or Expectant Parent classes, you practiced breathing techniques over and over. They got you through labor and delivery, didn't they? Why did you stop?

Watch the breathing of newborn babies. Observe their continuous easy breathing. Their abdominal breathing is automatic. At what point in your life did you switch from being an abdominal breather to a chest breather or perhaps to a shallow breather?

One more point: the lung has tiny blood vessels. Because of gravity, the lower lung has more circulatory potential, thus the importance of the deep breath. The inhaled air must be drawn into the lower lobes of the lung for greater oxygen pickup. Remember that oxygen equals energy.

When Should You Use Deep Breathing?

Use deep breathing frequently. It is wonderful. And it's free. You can use it during phone calls, folding laundry or ironing, during exams or any uncomfortable situation.

Feeling *overwhelmed?* — Deep breathe.
Children *fighting?* — Deep breathe.
Can't concentrate at work? — Deep breathe.
Children *pushing your buttons?* — Deep breathe.
Waiting to check out groceries? — Deep breathe.
Ready to *explode?* — Deep breathe.
Can't sleep? — Deep breathe.

You can do it. You can reclaim this natural skill and change your life. You can keep yourself energized.

Use breathing exercises preventively during the day. Consciously direct your breathing every hour you are awake. Tension flows out of your body as you exhale. Release your physical tightness and avoid accumulated tension at the end of the day.

Keep stress levels reduced through breathing skills. Why wait until you're so stressed out that you snap at everyone or burst into tears? Let breathing help you enjoy the moment.

Visual Reminders

Use visual reminders for directed breathing. There are several ways to do this. Buy colored self-sticking dots. They come in bright colors and can be purchased in a drugstore, office supply or variety store.

Plaster the dots around your home and at work. Put them in obvious places. At home, place them on the telephone, bathroom mirror and refrigerator. Be creative. At work, put dots on your calendar, watchband, telephone and at the top of your computer terminal.

Every time you see a dot, pause for a second to assess if you need to do breathing exercises. If an hour has passed, it is time to consciously re-energize. It is time to release your tension. You deserve to relax for a moment and regroup.

Use a red traffic light as a visual reminder. This should only be done in extremely light traffic. CAUTION: NEVER USE DEEP BREATHING EXERCISES IN POLLUTED AREAS OR CONGESTED TRAFFIC.

When you are at a stop light, and the air is clean, directed breathing is wonderful. After all, you can't go anywhere, so use the time positively. Do something for yourself. Deep breathing is also a great diversion if the children are fighting in the backseat. You have everything to gain from relaxing for a moment. Try several of these ideas and let the rhythm of your life reveal others.

Capture The Magic Of Breathing

Do you want more energy? Would you like to learn other exercises? Once you have practiced and become an expert in the calming breath, you are ready for more.

QUICK SIGH

There will be times when lengthy breathing exercises are not appropriate. Your desk at work might be located in a conspicuous place with a continuous flow of people passing by. If so, sighing can be powerful. It is quick, and you can use it anytime.

Test it out. Sit up straight. With your mouth slightly open, take a big sigh right now. A-haaaaaaa. Now, pause for three or four normal breaths. Try it again. A-haaaaaaa. Pause again and breathe normally. Try it a third time. A-haaaaaaa. That sigh can relax you. How do you feel?

Even a sigh breaks up neck and shoulder tension. When you sigh, your shoulders rise, forcing the tightness to break up. After three sighs, you should feel the release of muscle tension.

The quick sigh also helps chest tightness. When you go A-haaaaaaa, your chest is forced to expand, breaking up the constricted muscles. Every mother has time for this technique.

BLOWING TENSION AWAY

This skill combines visualization with deep breathing. Anytime you blend two techniques, the results are doubly powerful. If you are already using imagery, this will be easy. If you have never used it, then it is time to learn. Open yourself to energy and better health.

The dynamics from the calming breath exercise are used for this skill with imagery. While you hold your breath, rapidly scan yourself for tension. Scan from head to toe. Imagine your physical tension as a color. While blowing out the breath (exhalation), see the "colored tension" flowing out of your mouth and body.

1. Choose any color for your tension. It could be your favorite color, or if you view tension as negative, you could select a color you do not like. Many mothers choose bright colors in order to get the most vivid imagery.

2. Take a deep abdominal breath (three to four seconds).

3. Hold the breath (three to four seconds) while immediately scanning yourself from head to toe for tension. See the breath in color. Focus on the scattered color throughout your body.

4. Purse your lips and begin a long, slow exhalation (six to eight seconds) while seeing the colored tension flow from your body. Tension from the scalp, face and jaw flows out your puckered lips. Tension in the neck, shoulders and arms flows down your arms, through your hands and out the fingers. Tension in your chest, abdomen and legs flows down the legs, through the feet and out the toes.

5. Breathe normally now. Pause for 20 to 30 seconds while breathing easily. Then, if you need to blow more tension out, repeat this exercise.

Practice, practice. You can condition your muscles to release their tightness. This exercise only takes about 15 seconds, and it yields powerful results. Think about the relief you can have in one quarter of a minute.

This skill can be modified to help you deal with anger. If you tend to internalize rage, use the color red to represent this emotion. While holding your breath, color in the rage throughout your body. During exhalation, blow out the anger, visualizing the red flowing out of the body. Feel the relief.

OTHER BREATHING MODIFICATIONS

Combine deep breathing with tensing all your muscles, and then releasing. *Inhale* deeply, using your diaphragm. *Hold* your breath while *tensing your muscles* at the same time. For example: flex your toes up, bring your legs together, tighten your buttocks, pull in your abdomen, pull your arms to your chest, shrug shoulders up, and contract all facial muscles (frown, squint eyes, smile broadly and so forth). *Caution: Don't contract any muscles that are injured.*

Exhale fully while *releasing* all muscle contractions at once. Let your entire body go limp. Feel the difference this makes. Pause for 20 to 30 seconds while breathing normally. Repeat this exercise if necessary.

DRIFTING INTO SLEEP

Use breathing exercises to help you go to sleep at night. Lying in bed, focus totally on your breathing. Consciously direct your breathing toward a semi-deep, regular and easy rhythm. Inhale and exhale through your nostrils.

Become aware of your abdomen rising, then falling. Concentrate fully on this movement. If your mind starts to spin, redirect your focus to your breathing pattern. This can be a form of meditation. In moments you can be asleep.

You might add affirming phrases with your breathing. When you inhale, think "I am"; when you exhale, think "calm." Continue these comforting expressions. They are reassuring.

Or choose a one-syllable word that suggests relaxation and sleep. It might be "peace" or "calm" or any other word you select. Repeat this word over and over with your regular breathing. This is like a mantra in meditation.

ENERGY IN . . . TIREDNESS OUT

You can combine breathing, visualization and talking to yourself for energy. All directed breathing yields energy, but this exercise heightens the result. Imagine incoming energy as a bright light. See outgoing tiredness as a grey color.

Now, inhale, visualizing the bright light being drawn in through your nostrils. Think: "Energy in." Hold your breath while imagining bright light shooting throughout your head and body. Feel the stimulation of the dynamic energy. Exhale slowly through puckered lips. Think: "Tiredness out." Visualize grey tiredness being blown out of your body. Breathe normally five to seven times, then repeat.

Write one breathing exercise you choose to start now.

_____

_____

Building A Case For Directed Breathing

Breathing exercises can be an important part of your life. As mentioned before, focusing on breathing can be a form of meditation which brings on relaxation. Physiologically it can slow down the heart and pulse rate.

Yoga

Controlled breathing is one of the three components of yoga, along with intense concentration and a variety of postures. The postures or *asanas* are done slowly and in sequence, using gentle body stretches to prevent injuries. For 3,000 years, yoga has been used to achieve mental, physical and spiritual integration.

The benefits of yoga are astonishing. Blood circulation is stimulated, which increases the oxygen throughout the body. This results in energy. The stretching postures massage and stimulate the internal organs. Physical tension is released through the various stances, providing energy. The intense concentration on directed breathing acts to divert the mind, replacing or cleaning out the clutter. Yoga centers the mind and body, thus bringing balance and health.

Directed Breathing

Directed breathing can help anxiety and panic attacks. Panic attacks affect about five million Americans and are three times more common in women than in men. They are often triggered by a high stress event when women are in their twenties and thirties.

Victims experience an overwhelming sense of impending doom. Symptoms are sudden, such as pounding heart, chest tightness, dizziness, sweating, smothering sensation, difficulty breathing and a fear of dying. Causes are biological, genetic and psychological. The chemical changes in the brain produce the panic symptoms. Caffeine can bring on panic attacks in vulnerable women.

Along with drug and psychological therapies, physicians are teaching breathing exercises to relieve panic reactions. Diaphragmatic breathing has been found to intercept these attacks and ease the symptoms. Breathing is potent.

Breathing exercises are being recommended for other medical conditions. Asthmatics, for example, are being taught to use breathing exercises in combination with medical therapy.

Controlling the breath does several things: (1) it slows down the intensity of the asthma attack; (2) it reduces the anxiety and panic that accompany the experience; and (3) it increases the oxygen by improving lung efficiency, which eases the breathing.

In pain clinics across the United States, breathing exercises are being included in the treatment. They are significant for headache relief, chronic disease and musculoskeletal problems. Deep breathing can prevent or reduce muscle spasms. Directed breathing can release the physical tension, thus reducing pain. If you have a medical problem, talk with your health-care provider about breathing exercises.

Are you convinced of the power of breathing? If so, *make deep breathing a part of your life now.* Don't wait!

6 Good Reasons Why Children Should Deep Breathe

Can children use breathing exercises to help them cope with stress and anger in their lives? Yes, children can be taught basic breathing skills around age five.

Remember, though, that children have a smaller lung capacity than adults and their breathing is more rapid. The timing on deep breathing needs to be shortened appropriately. Here are six reasons why children should use breathing exercises:

1. To release anger and frustration.
2. To help children concentrate on homework and test-taking.
3. To reduce anxiety and hyperactive behavior.
4. To decrease stress and physical tension.
5. To help medical and psychological problems, such as asthma and phobias.
6. To ease them into sleep.

Write one reason why breathing exercises might help your child who is five years or older.

_____

_____

Some teachers have identified four important times for directed breathing: (1) when the children's behavior is hyperactive; (2) when students need good mental concentration; (3) immediately before a test; and (4) to keep classroom stress and tension to a minimum.

As a mother you can help your children learn breathing exercises. Model good "life tools" to help them cope in a highly stressful world. Children are very creative and can enjoy using their imaginations to blow away their frustration and anger.

The Magic Of Breathing

Make a decision now to incorporate directed breathing into your family's routine. Use breathing preventively every day of your life to reduce stress, break up tension and blow away anger. Most of all, use your breathing to re-energize yourself. Experience the magic of breathing now.

Model For Health And Energy

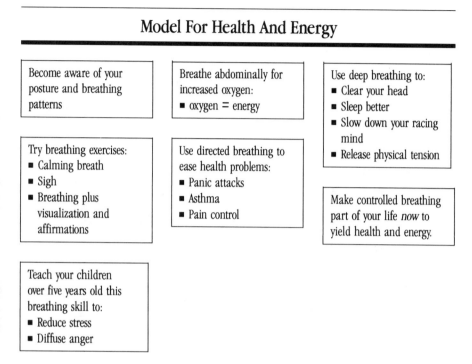

Become aware of your posture and breathing patterns

Try breathing exercises:
- Calming breath
- Sigh
- Breathing plus visualization and affirmations

Breathe abdominally for increased oxygen:
- oxygen = energy

Use directed breathing to ease health problems:
- Panic attacks
- Asthma
- Pain control

Use deep breathing to:
- Clear your head
- Sleep better
- Slow down your racing mind
- Release physical tension

Make controlled breathing part of your life *now* to yield health and energy.

Teach your children over five years old this breathing skill to:
- Reduce stress
- Diffuse anger

4

Are You Listening?

*I listen with empathy
and respect*

Mothers are fascinating creatures. They spend the first two years of their children's lives begging them to speak and the next 16 years trying to quiet them down.

Mothers never ask for help. They race around the house doing all of the chores, sizzling with anger because family members aren't helping. They say nothing, assuming others will automatically pitch in.

Good communication is a stimulus that provides family energy. It is a powerful force that moves a family forward or backward. It promotes bonding and connectedness and determines the quality of family life.

Stop! Look! Listen!

Three little words summarize good communication: Stop! Look! Listen!

Stop. Pause, cease what you are doing. Give full attention to the person speaking. Listen as much as you talk. Call a time out if emotions are escalating.

Look. Be aware of the dynamics of unspoken communication. Check out body language, your own and others'. More than 90 percent of your message is communicated through body language and your voice. Less than 10 percent is conveyed verbally.

Nonverbal communication is powerful. Silence, for example, is one of the most potent tools in communicating. The wonderful thing about saying nothing is that you never have to take anything back.

Eye contact or lack of eye contact also speaks. In America, eye contact transmits interest, caring and honesty. Your facial expressions and gestures are equally important.

Your mood can be communicated by the way you walk. A bounce in your step can convey energy and self-assurance. A shuffling gait can communicate negative feelings or a lack of confidence.

Check out the physical distance between you and the other person. Where is your comfort zone with your child, spouse, partner or co-worker? You might find that this varies with person, topic or mood.

Be aware of where you position your body during communication. This is key when talking with your children. Check out your stance before you start sharing. What level are you on? Are you standing, talking down to them? Or do you match their level? Do you get down on the floor or sit down to chat with them? Your position determines how they react to you.

Try to match your body language to what you are saying verbally because it is your body language that is understood.

Listen. Make it your priority when you communicate to channel your energy into listening. Never assume you know what the other person is saying.

Be A One-Minute Mother

Talk for 30 seconds. Listen for 30 seconds. Balance talking with listening. Talk. Pause. Listen. Reply. Do this in all of your relationships.

Listening has many surprising health benefits.

When you pause during a conversation, your blood pressure drops. When you talk, your blood pressure goes up. Imagine what happens when a mother screams. Newborn babies have been found to double their blood pressure when they cry.

Listen actively so you can hear and assess the feelings behind the words. Acknowledge feelings. Ask questions to clarify the message, and restate it to check your listening skills.

Try these two steps to active listening:

1. Identify and evaluate your child's feelings.
2. Repeat the message and acknowledge feelings. For example:

Child: "Brian is always picking on me. He wants to fight all the time."

Mother identifies feelings of frustration and anger.

Mother reflects back: "Zachary, I can see you are upset. It sounds as though you are angry because Brian is always picking fights with you."

Enrich Your Relationships

When you actively listen and reflect back, it enriches your relationship. The other person feels heard and understood, and communication opens up. Try it. It works.

List one message you heard from your child today.

_____

_____

What were the feelings?

_____

_____

Did you acknowledge those feelings?

_____

_____

What did you say back?

_____

_____

Blocks In Communicating

Your verbal messages can be ineffective or blocked. Consider four variables:

- Timing
- Environment
- Emotions
- Gender differences

Take these factors into account. They can help your message or block your effort to communicate. (See Figure 4.1)

Timing Is Everything

Choose the right time to talk. You might be exhausted at the end of a busy day. You could be irritable. You might be reactive. Your blood sugar could be low. (See Chapter 7.) This is the wrong time to discuss serious family topics. Have a snack, rest, then talk.

Keep timing in mind with the children. They are tired early in the morning, after school or at bedtime. Discussing important subjects at these times will backfire. You can discuss issues after they get refreshed.

Timing is key when you are settling family problems. Family conflicts should not be negotiated at mealtime or at bedtime.

Mealtime

You can make mealtime a positive social time for connecting with each other. Eat slowly. Take turns talking. Use this occasion to catch up with and nurture each other. Families with older children may find that mealtime

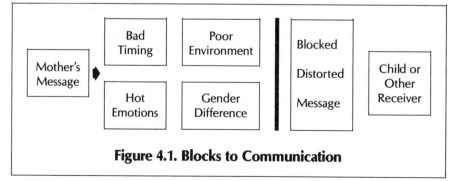

Figure 4.1. Blocks to Communication

is their only chance for everyone to be together. Positive communication during a meal helps to digest food. Negative and conflicting conversations upset the digestive process.

Bedtime

End the day on a positive note by making bedtime a time for sharing. Ease family members into sleep in ways that are relaxing and that minimize anxiety and stress. Avoid confrontations.

Have you considered timing in your family communication?

_____

_____

List one step you can take to improve timing in family sharing.

_____

Environmental Influences

A poor environment hinders communication. Noise is a major factor in sabotaging verbal sharing. Pause occasionally during conversations to assess how many noises are going on at the same time. TV? CD player? Radio? Stereo? Headphones? Air conditioner? Washer? Dryer? Telephone? Appliances? Tools? Toys? Computer? Dishwasher? Traffic or other outside noises?

Noise distorts and blocks information that is being transmitted and received. The distance between you and the other person compounds the noise problem. Family members in different rooms or on different floors cannot communicate yet they regularly try.

Here are three good rules that will prevent disruptions to family communication:

- Do not answer the telephone during mealtime, family meetings or conflict resolution. Ignore its ringing or let an answering machine take the message.
- Turn off the television during these same times.
- Don't start a conversation until you are both in the same room.

Other environmental variables are also important. Consider the temperature of a room. Is it ice cold? Is it hot and muggy? What about lighting and odors? Is the overall atmosphere relaxed or tense? Do any of these factors detract from your communication?

List one step you can take to create a better environment for talking.

_____

_____

Hot Emotions

Overheated emotions can cause an automatic shutdown of listening. As emotions escalate, hearing diminishes for you and the other person. Issues get exaggerated, objectivity is lost and damaging words may be exchanged, words that can never be taken back.

Anger, hostility and defensiveness can trigger dirty fighting, when name calling, labeling or put-downs easily occur. Past situations are brought up. Third-party opinions are used as damaging ammunition. Personal attacks continue, creating a losing situation, and relationships are strained, if not destroyed.

Sibling rivalry can also get very emotional. Refuse to be drawn into the bickering and fighting when your children argue. Back off from being a constant mediator. Unless the situation is life-threatening, just say, "I am not going to be involved with your fights. Settle the problem yourselves. I'll be in the kitchen working if you need me." Leave the room.

Write one step you can take now to limit hot reactions between you and your child.

_____

_____

List one rule you can make for more effective communication in your family and relationships.

_____

_____

Gender Differences

The "gender gap" can cause misunderstandings and spark conflicts between you and your spouse, partner or son. Differences exist across the board, in the workplace as well as in your personal life. Male and female ways of communicating are dissimilar.

Males tend to base their communication on a need to provide information, solve a problem or make a decision. Men also communicate to achieve status within a group.

Females communicate to share and connect with another person. Women easily express thoughts, feelings and experiences as a way to network and gain support from others. Sharing is often viewed as one way to achieve intimacy with another human being.

At the end of a busy day you might need to share the day's happenings. You want a sympathetic ear. Unintentionally the male in your life may not give you the attention you need. He might limit the conversation or show more interest in the television or newspaper. These differences in needs can lead to frustration and conflict.

Making allowances for the differences between men and women can mean better communication. You can discuss each other's needs and compromise on how they will be met. Communication in relationships requires ongoing effort and commitment.

Write two ways you and a male in your life differ in your styles of communicating.

_____

_____

_____

_____

How can you lessen this gender gap?

_____

_____

_____

_____

Healthy Families Have R-E-S-P-E-C-T

What makes a family healthy? What enriches family energy? The answer is simple. Respect. Healthy families are able to:

- Resolve conflicts, share conversations and recognize individual uniqueness.
- Empathize with each other and encourage togetherness at mealtimes and at other special family times.
- Support and nurture self-esteem, share chores and seek help when necessary.
- Problem solve and perpetuate a positive attitude.
- Encourage realistic expectations and standards within the home.
- Clearly define family rules, care for each other and confer with schedules and needs.
- Trust and take time for each other, treat each other like good friends and teach through positive modeling.

Besides respect, healthy families have other special qualities. They settle family differences fairly, usually within 48 hours. A specific time for the discussion is agreed upon in advance, and sneak attacks are avoided.

Distractions are removed so full attention can be given to one problem at a time. Threats, accusations and sarcasm are not permitted. Each person expresses her or his point of view regarding the issue, and family energy is channeled toward negotiating and achieving an agreeable compromise.

How do you settle conflicts in your family?

_____

_____

_____

_____

Write one decision you can make to improve family negotiations.

_____

_____

_____

Healthy family members are assertive. They communicate with honesty and directness. Using "I" statements, they express their feelings and their needs, and they can say no without feeling guilty. Moreover, they do not allow their communication or behavior to compromise another human being.

Saying No

If you can say no when necessary to family members, friends and co-workers and not feel guilty, congratulations. You are most fortunate. On the other hand, if you are a yes mother, you may feel angry and frustrated with yourself. You may recognize the need to say no, yet feel compelled to say yes for several reasons: fear of disapproval, rejection or not living up to others' expectations. Saying yes may be creating havoc in your life.

Ask yourself:

1. Do I feel guilty when I ask my child, spouse or partner for help?
_____ Yes _____ No

2. Do I struggle to confront a family member, relative or co-worker?
_____ Yes _____ No

3. Is it hard for me to speak in front of a large group of people?
_____ Yes _____ No

4. Is it difficult for me to be assertive with authority figures like my boss or father?

_____ Yes _____ No

5. Do I lack confidence in taking risks?

_____ Yes _____ No

6. Do I feel used or manipulated?

_____ Yes _____ No

7. Do I believe that other people's needs are more important than my own?

_____ Yes _____ No

If you answered yes to three or more questions, you may need to raise your level of assertiveness. The world has changed. Today's multiple roles, excessive demands and time constraints have mothers taxed to the max. You cannot survive without being assertive and setting limits on demands of your time and energy.

Communicating assertively may mean the difference between energy and fatigue, health and illness. Remember, you have *assertive rights* as a mother.

- You have the right to express your feelings honestly and directly.
- You have the right *not* to be manipulated by your child, spouse, partner or relatives.
- You have the right to be less than perfect, to lower your standards and to make mistakes from which you can learn.
- You have the right to take time for yourself to re-energize as a mother and to be the healthiest you can be.

- You have the right to say no whenever saying yes stops you from achieving your goals.

4 Ways To Become More Assertive

If you are struggling with assertiveness, you can do several things. Take assertiveness training through your community college or community adult education program, and read books on the topic. In addition you can:

1. PRACTICE BEING ASSERTIVE

Start small and take little risks. For example, introduce yourself to a stranger at a parent-teacher group meeting. You might initiate a conversation with another woman in your doctor's waiting room or shake hands with a new employee at work. This is a beginning. Build up your self-confidence.

2. USE MORE EYE CONTACT

Ongoing eye contact is key when communicating assertively. It expresses your interest in the other person. Eyes are highly expressive. Try lengthening your eye contact a few seconds at a time.

3. USE MENTAL VISUALIZATION

In your imagination see yourself being assertive. Take yourself through an entire situation in which you wish to become more confident. Mentally practice assertiveness over and over and over. Use this mental rehearsal prior to any uncomfortable situation, such as meeting new people, asking your boss for a raise, confronting a co-worker, taking a test or challenging a family member. This technique is very powerful.

4. INCORPORATE "I" STATEMENTS INTO YOUR CONVERSATIONS

Take responsibility for what you feel or want. After all, you can only communicate your needs. You can't be responsible for the thoughts, feelings or actions of other people, and you can't speak for them or change their behavior. Try these statements:

"I'm exhausted. I'm going to rest for 20 minutes. Then we can talk about it."

"I can't help you now. Let me start supper, then we can work together while it's cooking."

"I'm too busy this week. Let me check my calendar. I'll get back to you tomorrow. Perhaps we can work on the school project early next week."

Other "I" statements can start out with:

I feel frustrated that _____.

I'm angry because _____.

I am unable to understand why _____
_____.

I get upset when _____
_____.

I love you but _____
_____.

Several things happen when you become assertive:

- Your self-respect soars.
- You gain more respect from other people.
- You lessen the ways you are manipulated.
- Your increased confidence opens up new opportunities.

Your family might not like it when you start asserting yourself. Don't expect a standing ovation. Some family members will be supportive and others won't. Your children might be upset when they experience a loss of control in manipulating you.

Stay determined and reinforce your need to be honest and direct with your family. Emphasize that it is just as important for them to express their needs as it is for you. Encourage talking from the heart.

Do you need to be more assertive as a mother?

_____

_____

If yes, write one skill or technique you can use today to work toward assertiveness.

_____

Communication Can Be A Catalyst

Your family energy flow can be activated and sustained by . . .

1. Equalizing communication among all family members.

2. Using a team approach to define family rules and decisions.
3. Understanding the power of touch as a communicator.

Value the sharing of every family member. Evaluate the communication that takes place in your family right now. Who talks? Who doesn't. Visualize family communication as a wheel that provides energy. Use the wheel to complete this exercise on family communication. (See Figure 4.2)

1. Place the name of each family member on the spokes of the wheel.
2. Rate each person on her or his level of family communication in the past six months. Use a scale of 1 to 5. Number 1 represents poor communication; 5 indicates good and ongoing communication.
3. Draw a line through each spoke to define the member's level of communication.
4. Connect the lines on the spokes.
5. Study the drawn wheel.

Are the spokes of the wheel of equal length? Is the wheel balanced, or is it lopsided? How do different members match up? Is there an adult or child who monopolizes conversations? Who talks the most? Who talks the least? Do you have teenagers? Is there a difference between your adolescent and your other children? How severe is the inequity? Do changes need to be made?

If your wheel is highly irregular, consider how you might encourage more equal communication. For instance, you might increase the fre-quency of family meetings and rotate who leads the meetings and who starts sharing first. You may have to time or otherwise limit the talkers. Set ground rules first that everyone understands.

You might give special attention to those members who communicate infrequently. Listen to them more intently, acknowledge their feelings, ask more questions, give them more eye contact or increase your time alone with them. Keep in mind that family members differ in their need and desire to communicate. There will always be some discrepancy.

My family communication wheel shows that

_____

_____.

I could equalize sharing by

_____

_____

_____.

_____

The Jekyll-And-Hyde Switch

Adolescence is a mysterious time when children go through bewildering changes. The talkative child goes to bed only to emerge an uncommunicative stranger in the morning. This personality shift hits a family faster than a hurricane. As a mother you can be highly challenged by the changes.

Their silence is compounded when their bedrooms become a haven. They communicate by closing the door. Signs like "Please Knock" are posted. You feel unwelcome. Their deafening music bounces off the walls throughout the entire house, and the telephone becomes their lifeline. Endless hours are spent communicating with their peers. Secrecy becomes all im-

portant. Their communication with you is sometimes limited to one-word grunts, slang or defensiveness.

Hang in there. This too shall pass, and you will survive. First of all, don't take their changes personally. You didn't cause them, so don't blame yourself. Understand that these changes in

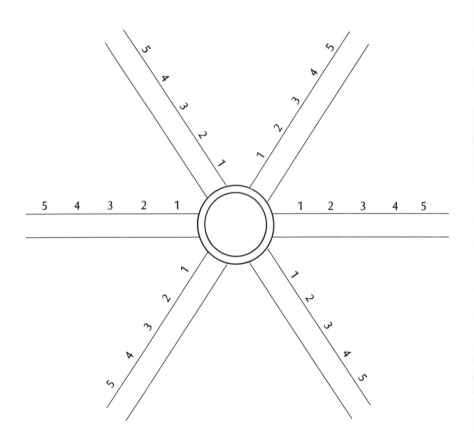

Figure 4.2. Family Communication Wheel

communication and swings of mood and behavior are physiologically induced and are part of a pulling away process that all teenagers must go through. It is their rite of passage.

No matter what, keep the communication going even though it seems one-sided. Let them know that you are there for them. Trust them. Become a better listener. Stop lecturing them, but do share honest concerns even though you feel they aren't listening. Tell them why you are troubled. Ten years later, they will still remember.

Show respect for their input, and ask their advice. Include your teenagers in some family decisions and let them know they are important. If you make a mistake, apologize. Your teen will respect you more if you confess to being human.

Ease up. Let them make some decisions, knowing that they may make mistakes. Try not to solve all of their problems, and see the difference between small and life-threatening situations. Stay on their team.

Most of all, schedule private time with your adolescent away from home. Once a week or twice a month, enjoy breakfast, lunch, an athletic game or a trip to the mall together. Do something meaningful with your teenager.

If there is an adolescent in your family:

Have you noticed changes in communication?

_____

_____

If yes, what are they? _____

_____

If needed, write one step you will take to improve communication and enrich your relationship.

_____

_____

_____

Rules And Consequences: A Family Affair

Involve every family member in regulating the group. Authoritarian approaches in the family are obsolete; a team approach is much more successful. As a group, you can define the rules and determine the general consequences for breaking them.

Keep your rules to a minimum so that each one counts. State them in a positive way. Write, post and explain each regulation. Modify the rules to reflect the ages of your children. For you as a mother, the most crucial challenge is to be consistent.

You might even consider having two sets of rules. One set is rigid, such as the time for bed on school nights. The other set of rules might allow more flexibility, such as how often a friend might sleep over.

Say Yes As Often As You Can

If you can say yes a lot, when you say no it has more impact and really counts. From birth to age 18, a child hears over 145,000 no's. Is it any wonder that no loses its power as a child gets older?

When rules are broken, confront your child privately, away from other family members. Create a relaxed, nonthreatening atmosphere, free of hot emotions.

Decide if the consequences set by the group are appropriate. If new consequences need to be defined, be open to the participation and input of the children, even if young. Listen. Write down their ideas. Children are often harder on themselves than a parent would be. Open up a discussion about possible consequences. If a serious problem has occurred, a contract, written and signed by the teen and parent, might be necessary.

Involving your children in rules and consequences teaches several things. They learn that actions have consequences, and they gain experience in problem-solving and decision-making. They also develop skills in communication and negotiation.

Who sets the rules in your family?

_____

Are all of the rules rigid or are some flexible?

_____

State one way you will involve the children more in rules and discipline.

_____

_____

_____

Family Bonding Through Touch

Touch is vital to human existence. It's a powerful communicator that connects and transfers energy from one family member to another. Babies may get more physical contact due to their daily care. In one study prema-

ture babies who were stroked several times a day had greater weight gain.

As children get older, they are touched less and less. By adolescence parents pull back, partly because teens shun open physical contact. This is unfortunate since adolescents need nurturing more than ever.

How can you ensure that necessary connection of touch? With a baby or toddler, rocking, holding and cuddling come easily. As children get older, cuddling, playing games and participating in activities assure that essential contact. An evening or bedtime massage is effective. With teens, a squeeze on the shoulder or pat on the back is reassuring.

Hugs Are Best

Hugs provide energy. Hugs are healthy. Hugs have healing power and provide a sense of well-being. Healthwise, they can lift depression, decrease anxiety and reduce stress. Hugs lower blood pressure. A hug communicates.

How many hugs have been exchanged in your home today? _____

In the past week? _____

In the past month? _____

How many hugs have you given to your children today? _____

How many hugs have you received today? _____ Yesterday? _____

List two action steps you will take to increase touch in your family.

_____

_____

_____

Start immediately to boost communication, the wheel of energy that connects and moves the family forward. Don't waste a minute. You can do it.

Healthy families in the future will make communication a priority. Busy mothers on the run will slow down, stop what they are doing and truly capture the message. Feelings behind the words will be recognized and acknowledged. Family members will be respected for what they think and feel.

Better family communication will be achieved because timing, environmental barriers and emotions will be considered. Successful mothers will be assertive, communicating more directly and honestly with their families.

Mothers will gain new energy as they relinquish some control and encourage more family involvement. As communication equalizes among family members and new rules and consequences are defined by the group, a new family closeness will evolve. Participation and communication skills will be essential to survive the next decade.

Start immediately to boost communication, the wheel of energy that connects and moves the family forward. Don't waste a minute. You can do it.

Model For Health And Energy

Use good communication to provide energy	STOP! Give your full attention	LOOK! Be aware of body language

LISTEN! Alternate talking with active listening	Improve communication: ■ Talk at the right time ■ Eliminate noise ■ Call "time out" with hot emotions ■ Understand gender differences in communicating	Promote family communication through: ■ R-E-S-P-E-C-T ■ Settling conflicts fairly ■ Assertiveness
Maintain family energy flow: ■ Equalize family member communication ■ Understand teenagers ■ Use a team approach to define family rules ■ Use touch to connect and transfer energy		Use good communication to yield health and energy.

5

Too Many Tasks, Too Little Time

*I make time every day to re-energize
myself and stay healthy*

Time is the greatest taskmaster. Mothers rush at 90 miles an hour, leaving many tasks unfinished. Where does the time go?

You may wonder whether you'll ever be able to slow down and stop doing so much, but you feel compelled to go on. You have the right to resist the compulsion to be two people.

In order to begin to take charge of time, you need to understand and appreciate the fact that you're human. Take one day at a time. Don't let tomorrow overwhelm you, and don't carry guilt from yesterday.

- Is time a problem for you?
- Are you trying to cram more projects into smaller units of time?
- Do you take on more before letting go of something else?
- Do you spend 30 minutes a day on yourself?

Mothers are deceived by time experts to believe that they can do anything and everything if they just try harder. In reality many mothers have already doubled their stress. Both single and married mothers with uncooperative families feel a tremendous stress overload.

Dangerous Adrenaline Highs

Some mothers become obsessed with time and are driven to squeeze more and more projects into less and less time. They develop a compulsion to be competitive. This compulsive behavior provides an adrenaline high that becomes addictive. These mothers experience great frustration and anger when expectations fail.

If you want to survive, you need a delicate balance. *You cannot work 24 hours a day.* For most mothers, there is no relief shift. Do you have people at home to take over for you?

You must be especially creative in order to guarantee your health and pace your energy. A rhythm of rest interspersed with work improves your ability to function efficiently.

Work Smarter

One key to managing time is to work smarter — not harder. Everyone has 168 hours in one week. How do you spend yours? Take control of your life by taking control of your time. Learn time management techniques.

AASSA

The letters AASSA simplify time management.

AA = Awareness and Assessment
SS = Skills and Strategies
A = Action

The Add-Deduct Principle = Awareness

The following exercise helps you become aware of problems and demonstrates the add-deduct principle.

A. Think about every new role or commitment you have taken on in the past three years. Examples might include new mother, caretaker of family member, new job, longer hours, chauffeur, religious involvement, new significant relationship, student, support group member or officer in a community organization. These are just ideas. List the roles you have taken on in the past *three years.*

B. Go back and in the parentheses write the number of hours per week it took for each role or involvement. Remember that each new position involves many added responsibilities.

C. Add the hours per week.
Your total is _____.

D. Now, write down each role or involvement you have resigned from or let go of in the past three years. In the parentheses write the number of hours per week you gained from giving up those positions.

_____ (   )
_____ (   )
_____ (   )

E. Add these hours.
Your total is _____.

F. Subtract the total in E from the total in C.
Your score is _____.

What did you find? Any score over five is too high. The greater your score, the more serious your time problem, and the greater your need to make immediate choices in your life. When you add roles, functions and responsibilities, deduct some, too.

If you keep adding more work hours year after year without letting anything go, you are going to be short of time and energy.

Adding new tasks and responsibilities requires letting go of something else. This is the add-deduct principle. You can jeopardize your health and relationships by pushing yourself too far. You need to make choices.

Write one thing you can let go of in order to achieve better balance and save time.

_____

_____

Check Out Your Log Jam

You must evaluate your use of time. For one week, log in all of your activities on the Time/Activity Log.

To save time making the record, use a system of abbreviations for completed activities, such as cc = child care,

Date: _____		
Code System		
Time of Day	Time/Activity Involved	Comments

Figure 5.1. Time/Activity Log

t = telephone, m = meal preparation and clean up, w = work hours, sc = self-care, i = interruptions, wd = washing and drying clothes, i = ironing and dc = domestic chores.

Expand the sample log to meet your needs. Make seven copies of the log, one for each day, and date them.

Down the left-hand column, Time of Day, list hours from rising until bedtime in 30-minute intervals.

List your activities and the time involved under the Time/Activity Involved column. *Record the number of minutes spent on each activity.* For example, self-care (sc) that takes 45 minutes could be recorded as 45-sc. For telephone calls and interruptions, add initials of the person. For instance, a 15-minute telephone call from Suzanne Ford could be logged in as 15-t-sf. Note if the calls or interruptions were social or job-related.

Add comments about persons or situations along the way.

Next, review the dates and analyze the seven completed logs, searching for patterns. Analyze your information in four brief steps:

STEP 1

Total the minutes you spent in each activity. How much time was spent in each category you coded?

Which two categories took most of your time?

_____

_____

_____

Are these reasonable lengths?
_____ Yes   _____ No

If no, write one change you are going to make now to gain time.

_____

_____

STEP 2

Look for time-wasters that rob you of precious energy. Focus on telephone calls and interruptions.

For example, how many phone calls do you make or receive each day? Who is involved? What is the length? Are they social or work-related?

List two persons involved with most of your personal calls.

_____

_____

Also note the interruptions. Who is involved? What is the length? For what reason did the interruption occur?

List two persons involved with most of your interruptions.

_____

_____

How could you change the frequency or length of phone calls and interruptions to gain more time?

_____

_____

Other time-wasters might include shuffling paperwork, failing to set priorities, being nonassertive, setting unrealistic deadlines, being unorganized, worrying excessively, procrastinating or being a compulsive perfectionist. Are any of these a problem for you?

STEP 3

Eliminate time-wasters. For instance, if the phone is a problem in your personal life, you can purchase an answering machine, let it ring, unplug it, have it disconnected or assert yourself and limit the length of your calls.

List two time-wasters you want to eliminate.

_____

_____

List one method for eliminating each time-waster above.

_____

_____

STEP 4

Use your prime energy time for priorities. When do you get your burst of energy? Is it once or twice a day? Do you get a second wind? When?

Some mothers are morning people. They bounce out of bed with high energy. Others experience energy peaks in the late morning, late afternoon or evening. The key is that top priorities can be accomplished faster and more efficiently during prime energy time.

Identify one or more two-hour periods during your day when energy is highest and you get the most accomplished.

Your prime energy time or times are

_____.

Study your log. What time of day did you start high priority tasks? Was it during your prime energy time? If it wasn't, could you change this pattern to save time? How? What time of day were you most productive?

State one project you are going to start tomorrow during your prime energy time.

_____

_____

Take Control Of Your Time

You can take charge of your time. Time-management experts say that for every one hour you plan, two are gained. Planning means taking control of time instead of letting time control you. Try the following skills and strategies. Take action.

- Make lists
- Set priorities
- Double the time estimate

MAKE LISTS

You can feel overwhelmed with demands and daily tasks. As your stress levels escalate, your ability to focus and make decisions diminishes.

Writing your goals on paper diminishes mental clutter and reduces stress. A daily to-do list provides a visual guide. The refrigerator (grocery and meal lists) and kitchen counter (projects list) are good for posting lists. Some mothers feel very proud when they can cross off completed tasks.

A pad of paper or a spiral notebook on a counter is better than a single sheet of paper, which is easily lost.

Paper and pen are also helpful in the car. Running errands or returning from the job, you can jot down one-word reminders.

A bedside pad and pen help to unload your mind during the night when insomnia, children's demands or unfinished projects might nag at you. Writing down the worry or undone task helps. You can then return to sleep, knowing the concern is documented.

List four tasks that need to be done this week.

_____

_____

_____

_____

SET PRIORITIES

You can set priorities by labeling the tasks on your list according to their values.

An "A" priority has high value and needs to be done soon. Example: Ashlee has her preschool physical at 9:30 this morning.

A "B" priority has moderate value. It may be important, but it has no immediate urgency. It can be done tomorrow or the next day. Example: The quarterly report needs to be redone this week.

A "C" priority has low value. It is neither important nor urgent. Example: The children's playroom needs reorganizing.

Put C priorities on the back burner. Let them go. Re-evaluate them every three to five days. Your C can jump to an A just as an A can drop to a B or C.

Now, go back to your list of four tasks. Evaluate each one. Label each with an A, B or C according to the value you decided on.

What did you find?

Write one A priority task you are going to start today.

_____

Focus first on A priorities during your day. If there are several A projects, subprioritize them according to importance and urgency: A1, A2, A3, A4 and A5. You may get to some B tasks, but remember, they do not need to be done. Forget the C priorities temporarily. Don't be compulsive about finishing every project written down.

Lists are rarely completed, and that's okay. Stress overload and severe time constraints block many mothers from finishing what needs to be done. To survive, remain flexible. Remind yourself that you are one person. Do the best you can, then let go. Tomorrow is another day.

DOUBLE THE TIME ESTIMATE

Doubling the time estimate is a key survival skill for mothers. Overload often occurs because of unrealistic expectations.

Women are frequently self-critical. They chastise themselves for not completing everything on a list. If five out of eight projects are completed, they focus on the three left undone, when in reality the list was humanly impossible.

Doubling the time allows for the unexpected, such as unplanned phone calls, interruptions, children needing attention, emergencies, equipment breakdowns, illness, lost car keys or traffic jams.

Take your prioritized daily list and roughly calculate how much time is necessary to accomplish each project. Then go back and double the time. This exercise brings reality to your estimate and reduces stress dramatically.

Write one task you need to accomplish.

How long should it take you? ____

Now, double the time. _____
This is the realistic estimate.

Cut Time Corners

Here are more strategies to help you save time and maintain your sanity. Make choices. Take action. Keep a calendar, schedule blocks of time for regular activities, plan meals ahead and make writing decisions.

KEEP A CALENDAR

Do you use calendars? If not, go get some today and start the calendar habit. Calendars help you to stay organized, thus saving time. Every mother needs a pocket calendar in her purse. You may find that a medium-sized monthly or yearly planner is also helpful. If you are using more than one, periodically compare and update them.

One large family calendar is necessary. Hang it in the kitchen, family room or hallway, where family mem-

bers can write in their activities, commitments and appointments for easy coordination. Transfer critical appointments to your purse calendar.

Schedule Blocks Of Time
For Regular Activities

Scheduling is a time-saver. For example, return phone calls from 11:30 to noon or from 4:30 to 5:00 P.M. Friends or clients are apt to take less time right before lunch or at the end of the day.

Other blocks can include study time for the children, chores, exercise, family-sharing and an evening ritual to prepare for the next day.

Evening Ritual

- To avoid morning chaos, schedule time each evening to prepare for the next day. Pack lunch boxes ahead of time with nonperishables. The week's sandwiches can be made Sunday evening and frozen. Or they can be made right after supper, before cleanup, then refrigerated until the morning.
- Set out clothes for the next day including accessories, socks and shoes. Let your children choose their own, depending upon their ages. They can help line up their jackets, scarves, mittens and boots.
- Put school necessities by the door in the evening. Organize backpacks. Put library books, parental notes, field-trip consents and homework inside the backpacks. Stack additional notebooks and textbooks next to them.

Reward Yourselves

You and your family can choose to reward yourselves for smooth-sailing mornings. You can vote on a trip to the mall, video rental, movie, special meal, making popcorn or playing in the park. These are all good incentives.

Write one activity you could schedule in a block of time.

_____

_____

PLAN MEALS AHEAD

You can cut corners by using these additional tips.

1. Let family members take turns choosing meals for a week at a time. You can draw up an initial list of 15 to 20 quick, nutritious meals for them to choose from.
2. Get the older children involved. Let your teenager with a driver's license do your grocery shopping. Have the older children share by starting dinner and setting the table before you get home.
3. Cook and freeze two to eight meals when cooking one. This saves money as well as time. Spaghetti sauce, taco sauce, barbecues, homemade soups and casseroles all freeze well. Make stacks of lean hamburger patties in advance. Remove meals from the freezer on Sunday and Tuesday nights, and let them defrost in the refrigerator. You'll be set for the week.
4. When family members are stressed and hurried during the week, choose quick and nutritious meals. Refuse to prepare those large dinners promoted in

women's magazines. Instead, prepare a tuna melt (ten minutes). Start by preheating the oven to broil.

- Children can set the table and remove needed items from the refrigerator while you drain the tuna.
- In the oven, lightly toast whole-wheat bun halves on both sides. This may only take seconds if the oven rack is close to the broiler.
- Place tuna on toasted halves and one slice of low-fat skimmed mozzarella cheese per half. Slip under the broiler and turn the oven off. Remove when the cheese is melted.
- Serve tuna melts with apples, raw carrots and a glass of milk. The fruit is the dessert.

Write one meal saver you can start now to save time.

_____

_____

MAKE WRITING DECISIONS

Writing letters and sending greeting cards may be difficult to get to today. Here are some budget and time shortcuts:

- Buy packaged all-occasion cards or obtain three months of greeting cards at 40 percent off at discount stores or through catalogs. Keep get-well and sympathy cards on hand.
- Keep a book recording all birthday and Christmas cards you send.

- Address greeting cards a month in advance. Leave envelopes open for last-minute notes, and note the date to mail the card where the stamp goes. You can also write the person's name in color on your calendar as a reminder.
- Write postcards instead of letters.
- Send Christmas postcards, not cards. Be highly selective to whom you send.

State one writing decision you can make to save time.

"Swiss Cheese" That Large Project

An excellent time-management strategy is to break a large project into manageable parts that can be done one at a time. This strategy reduces stress and prevents the feeling of being overwhelmed.

Major events such as Christmas, a graduation open house, work project, daughter's wedding, garage sale, birthday party and all kinds of family get-togethers are meant to be enjoyed, and they can be if you're organized. You don't need to be stressed out.

Step back. Get objective. Poke small holes in the project. Use the "Swiss cheese" method and tackle one task at a time. (See Figure 5.2)

List Tasks

List every task essential to complete a large project. Write those tasks horizontally in logical sequence and draw boxes around them. At the end of the sequence draw a large box to represent the completed project. Write in the name of the project and its completion date.

Assign Deadlines

Assign a realistic deadline to each necessary task. Keep in mind that big undertakings take weeks or months to complete.

Enter the deadlines in your purse calendar. Keep copies of your chart on your desk or on your refrigerator to remind you to check on tasks and stay on target.

Honor Deadlines

Stick to the deadlines. Complete each component as designated to avoid being overwhelmed. Continue to poke holes in the big project so that when the final deadline arrives, the job is finished. This process prevents procrastination and offers a realistic deadline to accomplish a major goal.

Task	Task	Task	Task	Task	Large Project
Deadline	Deadline	Deadline	Deadline	Deadline	
					Deadline

Figure 5.2. "Swiss Cheese" Method

Nurture Yourself —
The Rest Will Follow

How about taking time for yourself? Replenishing your energy stores is vital to motherhood. You are more productive and efficient when you have an ongoing flow of energy.

If you don't re-energize yourself, you will experience high stress levels and anger toward those you love. Giving, giving, giving, without any return, can make you resentful, and can teach others in your family to be takers, not givers.

You might feel like screaming, "I don't have time for myself! I'm too busy taking care of everyone else!" Watch out for this attitude. If you don't care for yourself, who will? What good are you to your family if you are sick or debilitated? You can't be there for the children and others unless you take care of yourself first. Forget guilt. *Don't ever feel guilty for staying healthy.*

Time For Yourself

Taking time for yourself is essential for a healthy lifestyle and positive relationships. Children need a break from a mother and vice-versa. You can model self-respect by pausing to nurture yourself.

Be creative in finding time for yourself. After the children are in bed, take a luxurious bath with candle-light, soft music and aromatic oils. Get up 30 minutes earlier than anyone else for special nurturing in the morning. In the evening, have the babysitter or child-care center keep the children 30 minutes longer. Use the extra time to read, meditate, lie on your back in the grass, take a little walk — whatever makes you feel special.

Find time for yourself and your spouse or significant other. Exchange children with another mother for one hour several times a week. Take an exercise class before returning home from school or work.

In the past month, you took _____ minutes for yourself every day. Is this enough? Can you do better?

List one action step you can take *now* to guarantee yourself a time to re-energize every day.

_____

When are you going to start?

_____

State one time-management skill or strategy you are going to use *now* to get control of your time and your life.

_____

When are you going to start?

_____

Congratulations! You are taking charge of your life.

Model For Health And Energy

A = Awareness:
- Let go of some roles if you add new roles (the add-deduct principle)

S = Skills:
- Make lists
- Set priorities
- Double the time estimate

S = Strategies:
- Use calendars
- Schedule blocks for activities
- Make meal and writing decisions
- Swiss cheese large projects

A = Assessment:
- Analyze your Time/ Activity Log
- Eliminate time-wasters
- Do top priorities in your prime energy time

A = Action:
- Use skills and strategies
- Take time to re-energize yourself

Control your time and your life to yield health and energy.

6

Mind Over Matter

**I take charge of my mind
to protect my energy resources**

Your mind is a powerhouse that can be your best friend or your worst enemy. It can coach you to heights of success or drive you to failure. Your internal dialogue and thoughts impact your energy levels.

Picture your energy resources as a bank. Positive self-talk deposits energy and provides stimulation. It motivates and refreshes you, brings renewal and makes you healthy. Your bank reserve swells when your inner words affirm you.

On the other hand, negative thoughts siphon off your energy reserves. Once set in motion they can become chronic destructive drainers of energy that deplete your bank.

Self-Talk — You're In Charge

When was the last time you listened to the chatter in your head? Your self-talk helps determine who and what you are, so it is worth paying attention to.

Listen

When you listen to yourself, what do you hear? Is your inner voice directing you in a positive way? Are you saying constructive things, such as "I'm going to impress them in my job interview today" or "I've had a rough week, but I'm going to make it." Positive messages propel you forward in life.

On the other hand your negative messages drag you down. They immobilize and exhaust you. They even can shove you backward. If you say, "I can't stand this job one more day" or "I'll never be able to change myself," you set yourself up for defeat. Your expectations in life are determined by your inner dialogue.

Where It Began

How did your self-talk evolve? A lot of what you say to yourself today stems from messages you received as a little girl. From the day you were born, the people closest to you played a very important part in shaping your "chatterbox." Over many years, especially during your early development, their comments touched you and were stored in your brain. Some comments may have developed into long-running mental tapes and may have been negative and hurtful:

"Can't you do anything right, like your sister?"

"I knew you wouldn't amount to anything."

It wasn't just your parents who influenced your programming. Messages may have come from anyone or anything.

Understanding how your self-talk

developed is important. Many mothers grew up in dysfunctional homes. They may have suffered varying degrees of mental, emotional, physical or sexual abuse, or perhaps alcohol and drugs were a problem. Some of the hurt may have been subtle, some overt. Acknowledging this history is important in healing. Although you were not conscious of or responsible for this programming as a little girl, as an adult it is different.

Make New Choices

Now you can choose to get help to make changes in your life. You can make your self-talk and thoughts work for you, not against you. It isn't easy. It takes time. But with help, you can do it. Professional support may be necessary. Self-help groups (see Appendix), classes and other community resources can also help you make it. Your inner chatter can be constructive, rather than destructive.

Flash back to this morning, when you first looked in the mirror. What did you hear your inner voice say? Write out the comments.

_____

_____

Were the phrases positive or negative?

_____

Did the comments work for you or against you?

_____

Your inner voice often surfaces when you are most vulnerable. The chatter might hit when you are looking at yourself in a mirror, meeting someone very important for the first time, taking an exam or interviewing for a job. Your mind knows just when to get to you.

There are many other reasons why you need to take charge of your inner talk. Your chatter becomes part of your belief system, influencing your attitude daily. If you have a negative mind-set, your mood will be lousy and you will act accordingly. Think about how your relationships are affected.

Take charge *now*. Learn to "engineer" your mind to protect your energy and get ahead in life.

Catch! Intercept! Rephrase!

Remember three little words that can change your life:
Catch. Intercept. Rephrase.

CATCH YOURSELF

Throughout the day and for at least two weeks, monitor your inner dialogue. See if your self-talk is positive or negative and how much of each there is.

Make a commitment to check your dialogue on the hour when you are awake. For example, tune in to your chatterbox at 8:00, 9:00 and 10:00. Pay attention to your inner voice. Even if you listen for a few minutes, you can make a dramatic evaluation of the direction of your inner talk.

Write It Down

If possible, write down your observations. This would be helpful be-

cause it is difficult to remember those assessments. At work you might have a code: use + for positive self-talk or - for negative.

At home, where you have more privacy, you can be more elaborate. Jot down some actual phrases you hear. Keep a spiral notebook. You might even do some journal writing in the early evening or after the children are in bed.

Monitor Your Moods

Expand your assessments. In addition to documenting the self-talk, write your thoughts and feelings for the day. Elaborate on your mood swings and how they impacted your behavior.

Review your notes, looking for patterns. Become aware of the debates going on in your head. Did you consistently use negative words such as "I can't," "I couldn't," "I won't" or "I'll never"? Did you constantly put yourself down?

Determine approximately how much of your dialogue was positive, how much negative. Note your attitude or mood problems connected with your negative self-talk and negative thinking. Some mothers have three-fourths of their thoughts working against them.

After two weeks of monitoring your self-talk, answer these questions.

Your repeated, self-defeating words (i.e., can't, couldn't, won't, never) were:

Your average positive to negative self-talk ratio was _____ percent to _____ percent.

Your overall attitude was:
(Check one)
_____ Poor   _____ Fair
_____ Good   _____ Excellent

If your attitude was good or excellent, congratulations. You are a very special mother, and your family is reaping many rewards. If your attitude was poor or fair, you need an adjustment. Read on.

INTERCEPT YOURSELF

The earlier you can interrupt your negative patterns, the better it is and the easier to do. You can refuse to allow negative dialogue and thoughts destroy you. You can intercept your old mental tapes. It isn't easy, but you can do it.

You can stop your thoughts in four brief steps:

- **Listen** to your mind. Be aware of your thought process by monitoring it periodically throughout the day. Notice immediately if an unwanted dialogue or negative thought is taking over your mind.
- **Shout stop!** If you are alone, yell loudly. If you are around other people, shout internally. Be emphatic when you shout.
- **Use imagery.** Combine the shout with an image. Visualize a stop sign rapidly coming toward you. Bring it right up to your face. See the big white letters S-T-O-P on the red sign. Use the two techniques (the shout plus the image) to make this skill doubly powerful.

- **Divert** your mind immediately. Instantly count up or down, deep breathe, imagine a pleasant scene, play music, go for a walk . . . replace the unwanted thought with positive messages. You have many choices.

Your mind needs to be stopped as well as diverted; otherwise, it will continue to ramble on and upset you. If anxiety or unwanted thoughts or self-talk try to take over again, emphatically repeat the steps above. Repeat, repeat this technique until your mind understands you are in charge.

Skills take commitment and practice. If this tool doesn't work the first time, try it again. Don't give up. It may take days, weeks or months to feel in control. Remember, breaking a conditioned cycle takes time. Persist. The rewards are worth the effort. As a busy mother you cannot afford to let your mind drain you of precious time and energy.

REPHRASE THE NEGATIVE

Rephrase negative messages immediately. Choose to restate negative words more positively instead of allowing your mind to ramble on in a destructive fashion. Start a reconditioning process. Yes, it is challenging, but it can be done. Retrain your mind. You don't have to believe the positive messages. Your mind will accept them over time. Communicate to your mind that the old messages will not be tolerated.

For example:
Catch the negative self-talk: "I'll never get everything done today."

Intercept: "Stop! I refuse this kind of talk!"

Rephrase: "I have accomplished three tasks today. I'm human. I will complete top priority tasks and let the rest go."

Try it yourself:

Catch yourself: "I can't relax and take time for myself."

Intercept: _____

Rephrase: _____

Was that hard to do? With practice it gets easier. You might say, "Motherhood requires energy. I deserve to be healthy for my sake as well as for the sake of my family. I choose to take time for myself to recharge my batteries and to be a more functional mother."

Try another one:

Catch yourself: "I couldn't possibly get that job."

Intercept: _____

Rephrase: _____

Your phrasing might sound like this: "I am a good worker. My credentials are as good as anyone else's. My skills are current. I am confident. I believe in myself. I'm going for it."

Keep At It

Changing your self-talk takes time. A lifetime of conditioning can't be changed by rephrasing a few sentences. Your mind can't be engineered in an hour, a day, a week or a month. Your change, growth and development are for a lifetime.

Take an "attitude check" periodically during the day. If you're getting down, say, "Up your attitude." Reflect on a positive event of the day, laugh or count your blessings. This might be all that you need to get back on track.

Distortions Of The Mind

Your highly creative mind loves to play little tricks. It can easily exaggerate and distort. It can turn a small incident into a family crisis, so watch out for the games it plays. When you are under stress, you lose perspective on what's happening and may not be objective. What you think is happening may not really be happening, but your mind has made it so.

Anxiety

Stress triggers anxiety. As anxiety and nervousness build, you lose your ability to think clearly. You jump to conclusions as your mind blows everything out of proportion. A small glass of milk, spilled by your toddler, becomes a flood on the carpet. You explode like a bomb.

Your mind plays other games when you are highly stressed. You can feel confused, indecisive and end up missing appointments and deadlines. You may feel irritable, touchy and subject to angry outbursts; depressed, anxious and unable to sleep.

Stop Saying "Must" And "Should"

Stress sometimes results from the mind's use of certain words, such as "must" and "should." Use these words sparingly.

Read these two phrases:

"I *should* spend more time with the children."

"I *must* get more done in my day."

Do you feel the stress created by these two little words? Monitor yourself to see if you use should and must too much in your dialogue. You can actually lower your stress as a mother by not using stress-filled words.

Check if you use the words should or must:

_____ Never

_____ Occasionally

_____ Most of the time

_____ Constantly

If you checked "most of the time" or "constantly," write one step you can take now to eliminate these words from your mind.

_____

_____

_____

The Energy Drain From Worry

Most mothers worry. In fact, certain concerns are justified and may be beneficial because they provide a focus for problem-solving.

Yet too many mothers have permitted excessive worrying to take over their minds. They have developed an obsessive pattern and are incapable of distinguishing between a worry and a real concern. The energy drain from unnecessary worry is enormous.

Women worry more than men. They tend to dwell on an idea longer, maybe because they've been conditioned to feel responsible for everyone.

How much worry is valid? Probably 5 percent. That means that 95 percent of your worries never materialize the way your mind has blown them up to be. Because most of the time spent worrying is wasted, you can resolve to direct that energy into problem-solving or some other activity. You don't have to waste time, sleep and energy. It's your choice.

Obsessive worrying is counterproductive, ineffective and all it produces is misery. It triggers anxiety, a sense of helplessness and loss of control. By worrying unnecessarily you choose to jump on the never-ending worry-go-round. (See Figure 6.1)

Riding the worry-go-round is easy . . . once you get on. If you have a worry and you choose to dwell on it, you can blow it up to any proportion you want. Remember, your mind is very creative. *Dwelling* exaggerates the original concern.

Exaggeration Creates Anxiety

Exaggeration makes the mind go wild. Your mind loves to stretch and build on an idea. Before you know it you've lost all perspective. The original concern will have been so inflated that your thinking is no longer rational. This exaggeration triggers anxiety.

Your anxiety is based not on reality, but on the distortion in your mind. Apprehension builds as you continue to dwell on the worry, causing many things to happen.

The prices paid for excessive worrying are tremendous. Energy is drained out of your reserve while you ride the worry-go-round. Sleep is not possible, you are robbed of precious time. Your ability to function as a

Figure 6.1. The Worry-Go-Round

mother is decreased because of this preoccupation. All of these losses create more anxiety.

Your anxiety promotes more dwelling. An obsessive worry can develop, which repeats the cycle and keeps the worry-go-round spinning.

Are You A Worrywart?

Do you spend a great deal of your day or night dwelling on needless concerns? As a mother do you brag about how much time you spend worrying? Do you think it's funny? When does your worry become a problem?

Worry becomes a problem when it disrupts your life. It is a dilemma when you are losing time, energy and sleep. When your worrying is affecting your mental and physical health and interfering with your relationships, it is time to take charge and get off the worry-go-round.

Write four worries in your life.

_____

_____

_____

_____

Have any of these put you on the worry-go-round?

_____ Yes   _____ No

If yes, would you like to do something about it?

_____ Yes _____ No

State one way by which your worrying has interfered with your relationships.

_____

_____

_____

Keep a worry log in which you document frequency, topic, intensity and length of time worrying. Also note times of the day when you are more apt to worry. Keep the log for one week.

Evaluate your worry log. Do your worries center around just a few topics or many concerns? Are there noticeable times of the day or night when you worry more? What other patterns can you see? Are you ready for action?

Banish Worries —
3 Techniques

Choose one of these three worry techniques to banish worries:

1. Worry Categories
2. Worry Time
3. Worry Box

1. WORRY CATEGORIES

• Take one piece of paper. Write down all of your nagging worries. Let your mind flow and unload itself. Allow yourself plenty of time.

• Take a second piece of paper. Divide the paper vertically in half and horizontally at the top. (See Figure 6.2)

• At the top left, write the heading "Worries I can control. I can do something about them." On the right side, write "Worries I cannot control. I cannot do anything about them."

• Take your initial list of worries and put each worry under the appropriate heading. You either can or cannot control them. Some you can do something about, some you can't.

• Study the categories and the lists. Your longest list of worries might be under the right column. In other words, your time and energy are being drained by things out of your control.

• Make a decision regarding those worries you cannot do anything about:

  • Set them aside temporarily. Evaluate them in two weeks.
  • Accept what you cannot change.
  • Let go of them completely. Release them.
  • Refuse to spin the worries.
  • Seek professional help. Pull on resources for help.

• Problem-solve the worries you can control. Take each worry separately. Complete a list of solutions for each. Then write an action plan defining specific steps to deal with each worry. Seek help from your support system if needed.

• Implement your action plan on worries you can control.

2. WORRY TIME

• Block out a specific time in your day for worrying. Allow yourself 30 minutes (e.g., 7:00 to 7:30 P.M.).

Worries I can control. I can do something about them.	Worries I cannot control. I cannot do anything about them.

Figure 6.2. Worry Categories

• Initiate firm self-talk if unwanted worries spin around in your mind at other times. Say:
  "This is not my worry time."
  "I will deal with this concern between 7:00 and 7:30 P.M."
  "I refuse to worry about this now."
• Repeat, repeat, repeat this phrasing as needed. Also divert your mind. You might do a chore, turn on music, exercise or read.
• At 7:00 P.M. it is your time to worry. Set a timer. Turn the phone off. Relax in a quiet environment. Entertain all of your worries for 30 minutes. Let your mind go wild. Problem-solve your worries.
• At 7:30 P.M., when the timer rings, your worry time is over for the day.
• Apply firm self-talk. Say:

  "My worry time is over."
  "I will let go of my worries now until tomorrow evening at 7:00 P.M."
• Get on with your life. Repeat the firm self-talk if necessary.

3. WORRY BOX

• Label a medium-size container as a "Worry Box."
• Write down the worry as fast as your mind thinks it.
• Fold the paper twice, then place it in the container.
• Apply self-talk firmly. Say:
  "I have written down the worry."
  "This worry is gone for now."
  "I have let it go."
  "I will deal with it later."
• Repeat, repeat, repeat this phrasing if your mind refuses to stop spinning.

- Divert your mind through imagery or an activity.
- Select a time, daily or weekly, to review the worry box contents and problem-solve.

Going through the container can be humorous. You may come to realize that many of your worries never materialize and that what you thought was a big deal really wasn't. Your perceptions change over time.

PROBLEM-SOLVING

Ask yourself three key questions before trying to problem-solve worry: "Is this situation worth my time and energy?"

"Two weeks from now, will this issue really matter?"

"Does anyone care that I'm losing sleep and function over this worry?"

Writing in a journal, talking with a pet or venting with a friend are additional mechanisms for releasing worry and for problem-solving. Music, relaxation tapes, reading, watching fish in an aquarium, exercising or imagery all help to divert your mind.

Assess your caffeine intake if you have high anxiety, excessive worry or a racing mind. Caffeine escalates all of these traits and also disrupts your sleep.

Model For Health And Energy

Protect your energy
resources by taking charge
of your mind

Watch out for mind
distortions:
- Stay rational
- Detect stress-filled words
- Use "must" and
  "should" sparingly

Choose to act:
- Monitor your inner
  dialogue
- Make your self-talk work
  for you
- Keep a positive
  attitude and mood
  through positive
  dialogue

Get off the
worry-go-round:
- Put your worries in
  categories and
  problem-solve those
  you can control
- Choose a time to worry
- Put written worries in a
  worry box, then
  evaluate them

Remember three words:
- CATCH yourself in
  negative self-talk
- INTERCEPT this negative
  pattern (shout *stop,*
  divert your mind)
- REPHRASE negative
  messages

Take charge of your mind
to yield health and energy.

7

Eat Your Way To Energy

I eat right to pace my energy throughout the busy day

Try to imagine what it would be like to have the energy to meet the demands of the day and not be tired. You can have it! Visualize being recharged through nourishment so that you can do the things you need to do.

You can direct your energy in three ways:

1. Eat right for energy.
2. Limit dietary stressors.
3. Secure needed nutrients (vitamins and minerals).

Eat Right For Energy

It's easy to take charge of your energy by eating right. Eat a good breakfast, nutritious meals, healthy snacks and the right food at the right time.

Some mothers think they can lose weight by skipping meals, but they're very wrong. Not eating meals can shut down your metabolic rate, compounding your weight problem.

Fuel For Your Day

Start your day with fuel. You need this . . . you deserve this. Don't short-change yourself.

You can't run on empty. Could you start your car without gasoline? Insist on a good beginning to your day.

If you wake up in the morning cranky and irritable you may have low blood sugar. A healthy breakfast slowly raises your blood sugar levels and provides an energy pool for you.

Healthy foods include oatmeal with minimal sugar, high-fiber (low-sugar) cereals, low-fat and low-sugar yogurt, fruit juice, skim milk, English muffins, low-sugar muffins, whole-grain toast or an occasional egg.

Avoid refined sugar products like sugared doughnuts or sugared cereals that have up to 60 percent sugar. They can cause reactive blood sugar problems, which you don't need.

Do you have a problem eating first thing in the morning? Get up 30 minutes earlier. Pack a nutritious breakfast to eat on your way to work or while doing errands. Healthy, low-sugar muffins, whole-wheat bagels, a piece of fruit or whole-grain crackers with low-fat cheese (mozzarella) are good. Eat a small amount at home, then take the rest with you.

Kids Need Breakfast

Are your children eating a healthy breakfast and starting their day out right? Healthy eating is vital to your children's behavior and necessary for their learning in school.

List everything you ate and drank in the last 24 hours.

Breakfast _____

Lunch _____

Dinner _____

Snacks _____

Beverages _____

What did you find? Was your intake healthy? Was it energy-producing? Did you skip a meal? Did you eat fast food due to time pressures? How much water did you drink?

List one healthy food in your diet.

List one item (food or beverage) you are going to change now to be healthier.

Keep a diet log for a week for a more comprehensive assessment.

Snacks Can Be Healthy

Busy mothers on the run need healthy snacks throughout the hectic day. Snacks energize you and stabilize your blood sugar levels. They are vital if you have large gaps between meals.

Energy slumps within three hours after eating indicate a snacking need. Mothers with low blood sugar should eat selectively and frequently between meals to help steady their blood sugar levels.

Healthy snacks include carrot or celery sticks, low-fat mozzarella cheese, wheat crackers, low-sodium pretzels, rice cakes, yogurt, fresh fruit, popcorn (air-popped) or an ounce of turkey. Limit high-salt snacks.

Your children need healthy snacks, too. They also may have low blood sugar when they haven't eaten for a while and get cranky, tired and misbehave. Two or three snacks a day are essential for children. An after-school snack improves their mood and behavior, which lowers your stress level.

List the snacks you have in your house right now.

_____

_____

_____

_____

List one healthy snack you are going to try.

_____

_____

Mastermind Your Meals

You can mastermind your energy level by altering the chemicals in your brain with the food you eat. These chemicals impact your mental alertness, physical energy and overall function.

Carbohydrates

Carbohydrates (starches, sugars and many fiber foods) provide energy. They are converted into glucose for body fuel. Glucose is key for body, brain and muscle function.

A high carbohydrate lunch gives you a temporary boost of energy. But in excess, carbohydrates found in fruit, rich desserts, potatoes, pasta and salads can induce lethargy. They enable a brain chemical that has a calming effect and can contribute to afternoon sleepiness.

Protein

Some protein at lunch stimulates alertness and provides you with longer periods of sustained energy. Three to four ounces of tuna, chicken, lean meat or fish are beneficial. So are eight ounces of low-fat yogurt or cottage cheese, tofu, soybean-based foods, skim or low-fat milk or two ounces of low-fat cheeses. The key is small to moderate amounts.

These protein foods stimulate different chemicals that provide several hours of energy. These chemicals heighten your mental alertness.

Timing

Lunch is a strategic meal. Eat for energy and clear thinking. Avoid alcohol, which makes you drowsy and sluggish in the afternoon.

Smaller meals are healthier in the evening. The traditional large dinner is out. Don't tax your digestive system late in the day. This causes problems with getting to sleep. Also your biological rhythms slow you down in the evening. A small, nutritious meal is best.

You do need energy after dinner, though. Doing chores or helping your children with schoolwork requires you to be mentally alert and efficient. Eat a variety of foods.

You can direct your energy. Choose the right food at the right time. Make healthy choices for you and your family.

List one step you can take to direct your energy with food.

_____

_____

Limit Dietary Stressors

Some foods and beverages can drain your energy reserves and cause fatigue. They stress you out. Your body may respond differently to certain substances.

You may need to limit the following potential dietary stressors:

CAFFEINE

Caffeine in varying amounts appears in many beverages, foods and medicines. Coffee may have up to 108 mg per six ounces brewed. Decaffeinated coffee has about 3 mg of caffeine. Sodas have up to 65 mg per 12 ounces. Tea can have up to 90 mg of caffeine depending on length of brewing. Herbal teas have no caffeine. A one-ounce chocolate bar has up to 20 mg. Prescription medications and over-the-counter drugs may contain caffeine.

Limit Your Intake

Up to 250 mg of caffeine daily may not be a problem for most mothers. This is about two cups of coffee. Small amounts of caffeine may help some if you do not have a sensitivity to it. In limited amounts it can increase mental alertness and clarity.

Substance	Adverse Effects
Caffeine	Stress, insomnia, headaches, irritability, nervousness, fatigue, palpitations (racing heart), stomach upset, sweating, racing mind, inability to concentrate, irregular heart rhythm, breast tenderness, anxiety, addiction
Refined sugar	Fatigue, blood sugar swings, deficiency of vitamins and minerals (e.g., B-complex vitamins, chromium), stress, obesity, tooth decay
High sodium, high salt intake	Increased blood pressure in sensitive persons, stress, nervousness, fluid retention, irritability
High cholesterol and fats	Increased fatty deposits in arteries, increased risk of heart attacks and coronary heart disease.

	Caffeine Substance	Approximate Amount
Day 1:	_____	_____
	_____	_____
	_____	_____
Day 2:	_____	_____
	_____	_____
	_____	_____
	_____	_____
Is caffeine a problem for you?		_____ Yes _____ No

Because caffeine can trigger anxiety or panic attacks, mothers who are highly sensitive to caffeine may not be able to have any.

Caffeine can accumulate and can stay in your body up to eight hours. Thus it causes insomnia and keeps you from getting quality sleep. Also, if you sleep late, you may experience a caffeine withdrawal headache.

Reflect over the past two days, roughly calculate your caffeine intake, and fill out the box above.

What did you find out? Is your caffeine intake low or high? Do you experience symptoms related to caffeine?

If yes, list two problems you have identified.

_____

_____

_____

You can reduce your caffeine intake if you choose to do so. If you drink excessive amounts of coffee daily, gradually reduce the amounts. Brew "half-caf" with half caffeinated and half decaffeinated coffee, or just dilute your coffee. Alternate coffee with tea, hot water or other beverages. Use decaffeinated coffee in small amounts. Make sure it is naturally water processed. Change to tea, especially herbal teas.

Use caffeine-free carbonated beverages or limit carbonated beverages overall. Alternate caffeinated sodas with fruit juices or water. Increase the amount of water you drink. A glass of water tastes better with a little lemon or lime juice or an ounce of a carbonated drink in it.

List one step you can take to cut back on caffeine.

_____

REFINED SUGAR

Mothers have quadrupled their intake of refined sugar products in the past century. Women are now ingesting 100 to 120 pounds of sugar per person per year. A good deal of your intake is hidden, especially in processed foods.

Beware The "-ose" Foods

Read labels and look for words like sucrose, fructose, lactose, dextrose, glucose and maltose. Be careful of foods containing corn syrup or other sweeteners. Remember that substances are listed on labels in sequence according to their amount. The first ingredients have the greater amounts.

Low Blood Sugar

Your energy levels can be threatened by refined sugar products. Reactive low blood sugar can occur. This reaction is heightened on an empty stomach. (See Figure 7.1)

Refined sugar can cause a yo-yo effect within your body. Sugar products give you a rapid, temporary boost of energy as your blood sugar shoots up.

This sugar rush triggers the release of insulin from your pancreas. Insulin regulates your blood sugar. The pancreas may oversecrete because of the rapid impact from the sugar. This results in low bood sugar, and you then experience a rapid downer.

Low blood sugar affects you mentally, emotionally and physically. You may feel fuzzy, light-headed, moody, anxious and irritable. Fatigue, headaches and sweating are also common. You have pronounced "cravings for sugar" when your blood sugar is low. If you reach for more refined sugar, the yo-yo effect can start again.

B Vitamins

Excess sugar causes other problems for mothers. Processed sugar may have few or no nutrients, so your vital B vitamins and chromium (mineral)

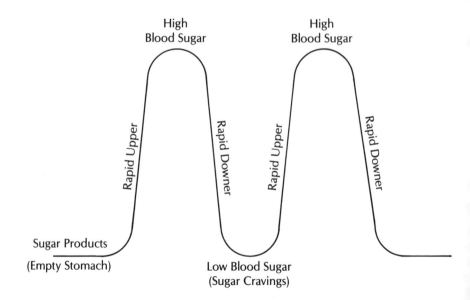

Figure 7.1. Blood Sugar Swings

are used and drained away. Deficiencies can develop.

The B vitamins are critical to your moods, emotions and nervous system. Therefore, B deficiencies affect you greatly. Irritability, mood swings, increased crying and depression can occur. Chromium stabilizes blood sugar levels.

Two things seem clear: (1) sensitivity to sugar is individual and (2) reactions depend on timing and what is ingested with the sugar. Sugar products ingested on an empty stomach or taken with caffeine or alcohol trigger heightened reactions. Small amounts of sugar taken after a large meal may not be a problem for many mothers.

Hidden Sugar

How much sugar is in products? A sweet carbonated beverage (12 ounces) contains 10 teaspoons, an average chocolate bar contains 7 teaspoons, a piece of chocolate cake (two-layer with frosting) contains 15 teaspoons, a slice of cherry pie contains about 14 teaspoons.

Read labels on everything you eat for the next two days. Roughly calculate sugar amounts.

You do need glucose for the well-being of your mind and body. Your brain is dependent on glucose; however, many women use sugar excessively in their diets.

If you choose to cut back on sugar and stabilize your blood sugar levels, you might try the following:

1. Eat three meals a day with three snacks, mid-morning, mid-afternoon and evening. Or eat five to six small meals daily. Don't snack on just complex carbohydrates like a banana and crackers. Try to have at least one ounce of protein. Protein is better in smaller amounts.

2. Replace refined sugar products with a higher fiber complex carbohydrate and a small amount of protein. Fiber and small amounts of protein help to stabilize insulin levels and

	Sugar Substance	Approximate Amount
Day 1:	_____	_____
	_____	_____
	_____	_____
	_____	_____
Day 2:	_____	_____
	_____	_____
	_____	_____
	_____	_____

Are sugar products a problem for you?   _____ Yes _____ No

slow the release of sugar, so they are good to eat.

3. Cut out caffeine, alcohol and nicotine because they all overstimulate the pancreas and adrenal glands. Caffeine and nicotine trigger adrenaline, which causes the liver to release stored up sugar.

4. Limit all sugars (white, brown, raw, corn syrup, honey, molasses and syrup). Avoid sugar products such as candy, cookies and cakes. If you need a small amount of a sugar product, have it after a meal.

5. Don't drink sweet carbonated drinks. Replace or alternate diet sodas with flavored water.

6. Seek medical attention if you react dramatically to sugar and sugar products. Keep a log of timing, sugar substances and related symptoms before seeing your health-care provider.

List one step you can take to reduce sugar intake if you suspect a problem.

Should you switch to artificial sweetners? No. Problems have been reported with some of them. *Be cautious.* Small amounts may not be a problem unless you have a sensitivity to them. Cutting back on all sweets is better.

SODIUM/SALT

Excess sodium or salt affects you in several ways. If you have severe premenstrual syndrome (PMS), excessive sodium can intensify your symptoms. Excessive sodium causes fluid retention. Your body and brain are both affected. Mood and emotional upsets increase.

A small segment of the population is sensitive to sodium, resulting in increased blood pressure. Salt is a stimulant and can trigger the stress response. A flavor enhancer, such as monosodium glutamate (MSG), can cause headaches and other mental and physical problems in sensitive individuals.

Sodium Every Day

Is daily sodium necessary? Absolutely. It regulates heart action and the water balance in your body. Safe and adequate amounts of sodium range from about 1,000 to 3,000 mg daily. Unfortunately, mothers often consume two to three times that amount.

Hidden Sodium

At least half of your sodium intake is hidden. You may add little table salt, but processed foods can have excessive amounts.

Read labels and look for ingredients containing sodium, such as sodium nitrate, sodium phosphate, sodium bicarbonate (baking soda), sodium ascorbate, sodium saccharin and monosodium glutamate.

Examples of sodium in foods include one medium frankfurter, 639 mg; one cup of canned spaghetti with meatballs, 1,220 mg; one ounce of American processed cheese, 445 mg; five pretzels (one ounce), 890 mg; a frozen turkey dinner, 735 mg; one ounce of chipped beef, 1,220 mg. Fast foods, canned foods and some prepared TV dinners can contain excessive amounts of sodium.

Log in your sodium intake for two days.

If you choose to reduce excess sodium, limit salt in cooking. Refrain

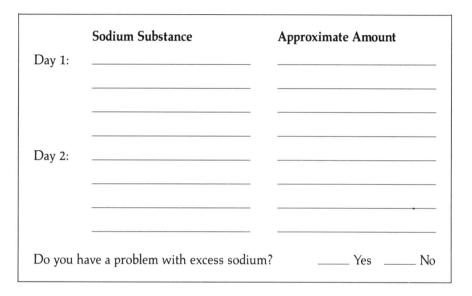

from putting the salt shaker on the table. Read labels and base your food choices on sodium ingredients. Use a palatable salt substitute. Cook with garlic (which offers many healthy benefits), onions or herbal seasonings instead of salt. Refrain from using MSG as a flavor enhancer. Refuse to buy salty snacks for your family. Avoid fast food, processed food and canned food.

List one step you can take to cut back on sodium if there is a problem.

_____

_____

_____

Watch Those Mood-Swinging Agents

Most mothers do not like feeling out of control because of their mood swings. In reality, however, it may be that your moods are affected by some of the substances you put into your body. Although most of these have already been discussed, it is important to state them again. (See Figure 7.2)

The mood-swinging agents are caffeine, sugar products, excess sodium, foods causing sensitivities or allergies (such as wheat, gluten, etc.) and alcohol. These substances affect mothers differently. What affects you might not bother another. Get in touch with your individual sensitivity.

- Caffeine: anxiety, irritability, depression
- Sugar products: mood swings, irritability, depression
- Excess sodium: irritability, mood changes
- Foods causing sensitivities or allergies: irritability, anxiety, depression
- Alcohol: mood-changing agent

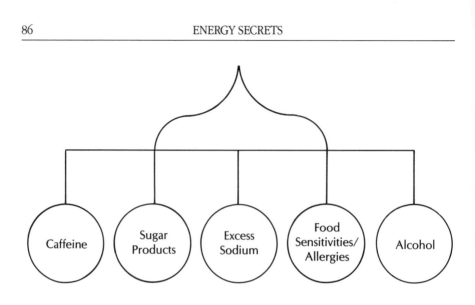

Figure 7.2. Mood-Swinging Agents

Your mood problems and stress levels can be lessened by making choices within your assessed diet. Your energy levels can be raised by limiting those substances that trigger stress in your body. If you suspect food sensitivities or allergies, consult with a nutritionist who understands the relationship of diet to moods and behavior.

Some mothers cut their stress level and PMS in half by changing their diets. By limiting dietary stressors and mood changers 10 to 14 days before and a few days into the beginning of your period, your premenstrual symptoms are often eased. You feel better and more in control.

Have you ever felt like a witch?
_____ Yes   _____ No

If yes, would you like to feel and act differently?
_____ Yes   _____ No

List one step you can take to limit a mood-swing and feel better.

Cholesterol, Fats And Women's Health

Heart attacks stand out as the number-one killer of women. Nearly half of all heart attack deaths occur in females. New studies are being designed to address this high-risk problem for women.

Diets high in cholesterol and excessive fats are stressors to women. High fat intake causes other problems beyond heart disease and may contribute to breast and other cancers.

Some dietary fat is needed for energy, but the American diet is excessively high in fat.

Cholesterol is a fatlike substance in the bloodstream. High levels of cholesterol and other fatty substances in your blood can build up plaque in your arteries. Over the years the arteries to your heart are narrowed and heart disease occurs.

State your current total blood cholesterol level: _____ mg.

If you don't know your cholesterol level, check with your health-care provider. Have your cholesterol level interpreted.

Several factors influence your cholesterol levels. Your diet is very important and is the one factor you can control. Your liver produces about 1,000 mg of cholesterol a day. Hereditary factors also influence your cholesterol level and the fatty substances in your blood.

You can become healthier by limiting high cholesterol foods and excess dietary fats. All fats are important, but it is crucial to restrict saturated fats (from animal sources).

MAKE HEALTHY CHOICES

Be heart-wise. Cut back all meats to three- to five-ounce servings (the size of a deck of cards). Limit heavily marbled and fatty meats, such as spareribs, high-fat luncheon meats or ground meats, bacon and sausage. Use only lean cuts and trim meats. Bake or broil foods and avoid deep frying.

Increase your intake of poultry (naturally raised) and remove the skin. Lean meats and poultry can have similar amounts of cholesterol, but poultry without skin may have less fat.

Increase your consumption of fish (commercially raised). Limit egg yolks to three a week, and watch your intake of cheese. Use low-fat dairy products whenever you can.

Whole milk (8 ounces) has about 33 mg of cholesterol and 5.1 fat grams, yet skim milk (8 ounces) has only 4 mg of cholesterol and 0.3 grams of saturated fat. This makes a difference.

Limit your intake of saturated fat from animal products (lard or butter) or such oils as coconut or palm oil. Use a fat-free cooking spray and non-stick cookware. Small amounts of olive, corn or safflower oil are okay. But limit margarine and avoid hydrogenated products.

Refuse to buy high-fat commercial crackers, deep-fried snacks or store-bought desserts such as cakes, mixes, pies and cookies.

Increase your intake of vegetables, fruits and high fiber foods.

Do you think that your diet needs an adjustment regarding cholesterol and fats?
_____ Yes   _____ No

If yes, list one step you can take to reduce high cholesterol and high-fat foods.

_____

_____

Secure Needed Nutrients (Vitamins And Minerals)

Vitamins and minerals are important to energy levels. Deficiencies affect your energy levels.

B complex and C vitamins are water soluble, so they must be replenished daily. They are depleted rapidly during high stress times. Other vitamins, A, D, E and K, are fat soluble and are stored in the body. Problems can occur if mothers take an excess of these in supplements.

Mothers are at high risk for vitamin and mineral deficiencies for several reasons.

- They skip meals, eat fast foods or eat little because of time pressures.
- They are often dieting to lose weight.
- They do not eat a balanced diet with a variety of foods.
- Their high stress levels or dietary stressors siphon off precious vitamins and minerals.
- They continue to smoke and to drink alcohol. Both of these block nutrients from being utilized.

Prevent Deficiencies

Deficiencies are common today. About one-third of all women in their reproductive years are iron deficient. Many mothers are deficient in calcium and vitamin B_6 (pyridoxine). Mothers on birth-control pills can also develop a B_6 deficiency. Also, women continue to smoke cigarettes, and smokers have a lower vitamin C blood level than nonsmokers.

Nutrients are different in today's food supply compared with 50 years ago. Variables that reduce nutrients are chemical fertilizers, early harvesting, boxing, transporting, storing and food processing. Lighting and air drying in grocery stores lower the nutrient value even more. At home peeling, canning, thawing, heating and cooking take their toll.

How can you ensure the greatest vitamin and mineral intake? (1) Mi-

crowave foods quickly. (2) Steam foods with a scant amount of water. (3) Buy from local organic growers. (4) Grow your own. (5) Limit vitamin and mineral robbers, such as dieting, stress, caffeine, alcohol, refined sugar products and smoking. (6) Choose fruits and vegetables with peels, such as bananas, oranges, pineapples, peas and corn.

Get your nutrients from a variety of foods. If you do need a vitamin/mineral supplement, check with your health-care provider. Take the supplement with a meal for better absorption and utilization.

Mothers' Special Needs

- Make sure you get adequate B vitamins. They help to stabilize your moods, emotions and nervous system. Use food sources such as grains, fortified cereals, sunflower seeds, fish, poultry, meat, dry peas or beans and milk products. Increase these foods under stress.
- Vitamin C stimulates your immune system, helps you cope with stress and is critical to healing. It is available in fresh fruits and vegetables, particularly citrus fruits, broccoli, cantaloupe, potatoes, cabbage and green peas.
- Iron, a mineral, is critical to your energy levels. Fatigue, anemia and a decreased immune system can result from a deficiency. Make sure that fortified cereals and breads, beef, eggs and spinach are in your diet.
- Calcium, a natural tranquilizer, soothes you in high stress times, helps PMS symptoms and is critical in preventing osteoporosis (even in your twenties and thirties). You need 1,000

mg of calcium in your diet daily, so include in your diet low-fat, low-sugar yogurt, low-fat milk products, low-fat cheeses, broccoli, beans, tofu, salmon with bones and dark leafy green vegetables.

• Vitamins and minerals are crucial to mothers, who need every ounce of energy they can get. Make sure you eat balanced meals, with a variety of foods, to assure getting these nutrients.

Do you think you are getting the vitamins and minerals you need?

_____ Yes _____ No

List one step you can take to increase vitamins and minerals in your diet.

_____

_____

_____

Model For Health And Energy

Eat right for energy:
- Breakfast
- Nutritious meals
- Healthy snacks
- Right food at the right time

Reduce risks of heart disease and cancer:
- Limit high cholesterol foods
- Reduce fat intake (especially saturated fats)

Cut dietary stressors:
- Caffeine
- Refined sugar
- Excess sodium

Let vitamins and minerals help you use energy from foods:
- Get your vitamins and minerals from a variety of foods
- Cut out variables that reduce nutrients in food
- Limit vitamin and mineral robbers
- Increase dietary intake of the vitamin B complex, vitamin C, iron and calcium

List mood-changing agents:
- Caffeine
- Sugar products ·
- Foods causing sensitivities/allergies
- Excess sodium
- Alcohol

Eat right to yield health and energy.

8

Energy Rx

I choose exercise to improve my mind, body and emotions

How about a prescription that costs nothing, builds your self-concept, improves your mental health and helps to prevent colon cancer?

That prescription is exercise. Exercise, you say? Ridiculous. Impossible. Think again; exercise is an energizer and stress-reducer with a written guarantee.

The fitness craze of the seventies and eighties turned many mothers off because they were led to believe that if they didn't run, jog or do high-impact aerobics for one hour, three to five days a week, they couldn't achieve health. So mothers gave up and stopped trying to exercise.

The guidelines set by fitness experts were an illusion. For families, but particularly for mothers, they were unrealistic in terms of time and energy.

The fitness movement over the past decades brought other problems. It promoted compulsiveness and produced addictive behavior in some people. It pushed competitiveness, some of it unhealthy. Exercise became performance-oriented.

Persistent excessive exercise also brought physical problems. Bone, joint, muscle and tendon injuries increased. Hormonal disturbances and infertility problems were identified. Today all this is changing, and moderation is in.

Exercise Redefined

Exercise is being redefined in the nineties. Overdoing is now seen as unhealthy. "No pain, no gain" is out. High-impact sports are approached cautiously.

A no-sweat approach is in, and moderation and low-impact aerobic activity are encouraged. Consistency and regularity are the important factors, not a fast pace.

Exercise Is Magic

Exercise is magic in its power to improve your quality of life. Its mental, emotional and physical benefits are tremendous.

It reduces mental stress and pressure. It promotes mental energy, improves memory and alertness and releases your anger. Exercise boosts self-esteem and self-image, which in turn, empower self-confidence — all important for tired mothers.

Physical activity alters your brain by releasing endorphins that improve your moods and attitude. Anxiety, panic attacks and depression decrease.

Endorphins released during exercise diminish mood problems. These morphinelike substances create a euphoric feeling of well-being. A mother who is physically active will say that she feels better after exercising. If she stops her exercise program, she misses that good feeling.

List one mental or emotional reason for you to exercise.

_____

_____

HEALTH BENEFITS

The benefits of exercise have been widely stressed over the past decades. A few benefits that are relevant to women need to be emphasized. Exercise stimulates your metabolic rate, helping you to burn off calories. Simply put, physical activity burns fat. This helps you to maintain or lose weight.

Physical activity firms your muscle tone and improves the flexibility and mobility of muscles and bones. It slows the natural loss of bone mass after age 35, preventing the "silent killer," osteoporosis. Weight-bearing exercise (e.g., walking, hiking, aerobic dancing, tennis), 1,000 mg of dietary calcium per day and estrogen after your reproductive years are three key ways to prevent this disabling disease.

Exercise improves heart and lung efficiency, circulation and lowers blood pressure. It increases high density lipoprotein (HDL), which is the good component of your blood cholesterol. HDL sweeps your arteries, preventing the buildup of plaque. A challenging exercise program prevents or delays heart disease.

Challenging physical activity also decreases insulin needs in your body. Thus, it may play a part in preventing diabetes. Three other important pluses for exercise are that it (1) prevents constipation; (2) eases minor aches and pains; and (3) is a natural tranquilizer, enhancing sleep.

How could exercise energize you? Count the many ways. Physical activity:

- stimulates you.
- motivates you internally.
- boosts enthusiasm and optimism.
- increases oxygen intake, thus improving mental, physical and muscular function.
- relieves fatigue by releasing tension in your body.
- clears stress hormones out of your body.

How does that sound? Could you use a little extra energy right now? Might you consider getting more physical activity in your life? A decrease in tension follows a brisk 10-minute walk.

List one reason for you to exercise.

_____

_____

List one way you would like exercise to energize you.

_____

_____

Sneak In Exercise

You can sneak in physical activity throughout your busy day. Use the stairs at home and at work. Park three to four blocks from where you are going. Force yourself to walk. You can do it, and you'll feel better.

Exercise At Work

Use one third of your lunch hour for a brisk walk. This is fantastic even if you can't do it daily. Two or three times a week is helpful. If you have a 30-minute lunch, take a brisk walk for ten minutes. If you have an hour, try 20 minutes. Fresh air and increased oxygen help you feel better. You'll be surprised at how energized you can be in the afternoon.

Use walking as a tool to build and maintain your workplace support system. Grab a colleague and set a goal. Make it fun. Clock yourself and work toward a reward. Treat yourself and your exercise supporter to a lunch or dinner once you reach so many miles.

There are brief moments of physical activity you can do at work. Walk to the restroom or copier more briskly. Get up and walk around your desk. Rather than calling, walk to another department to talk with a colleague.

These activities increase your productivity, stimulate your circulation and increase your energy reserve.

State one thing you can do at work to improve your physical activity.

_____

_____

List one step you can take to increase exercise or physical activity at work.

_____

_____

MAKE TIME FOR EXERCISE

Some mothers take a brisk walk or attend an exercise class before returning home for the day. Check with your community college or community adult education program. If you are a student, you can choose from among many classes. Swimming, yoga, body flexibility, aerobic walking, tone and stretch, weight training and volleyball classes are usually available.

Any activity helps. Some mothers work out at a fitness center, YWCA or health or athletic club. With stress relieved and in a better mood, you are ready to face the rest of your day.

Exercise At Home

For mothers who do not have the time or energy to leave their homes, dozens of ideas for increased activity are available to you. Home exercise programs are soaring, and television offers a variety of activity ideas.

Exercise videos are ideal because they provide flexibility for the busy mother. You can do one in the morning before leaving for work or at any time during the day if you are at home. Younger children like to participate.

If you prefer an aerobic program, choose an exercise you love that is also realistic. Get approval from your health-care provider. Start your program slowly, always using a warm-up and cool-down period for 10 to 15 minutes before and after. Learn to listen to your body for signals that you are overdoing.

Some mothers have a rowing machine or stationary bike. The cost of equipment varies. You can watch television with the children while working out on a stationary bike. You can even read or study while pedaling away.

A treadmill with adjustable incline and speed is popular. Cross-country ski machines are great. You can watch a video of a snowy mountainside and experience skiing down the slopes. This diversion is mentally refreshing, and you reap many rewards physiologically.

Stair and stepping machines are the newest to offer low-impact aerobics. Mothers who can't leave the home are also doing strength-training and bodybuilding. More homes are equipped with gyms, and trainers are even making housecalls.

Chores As Exercise

Make your chores count: trips to the basement to do laundry, vacuuming, dusting, sweeping, scrubbing and mopping floors provide you with exercise. Scraping paint, wall-papering and kneading bread give your muscles a workout.

Mowing the lawn, weeding, raking leaves and shoveling snow help. Climbing the ladder to wash windows or clearing out the gutters forces you to stretch. Don't curse the work; enjoy the opportunity for exercise.

Grocery shopping can be part of your exercise program. Park further from the supermarket to increase your walking activity.

List two chores that increase your physical activity the most.

_____

_____

List one step you can take to sneak in exercise.

Trade A Chore For Physical Activity

Examine your priorities. Let a chore go or do it less frequently in order to get more exercise. You can do it. Take a look at your domestic chores and how often you are doing them.

Are you compulsive about some chores? Do you do things that can wait? Are you a perfectionist, obsessed by your own standards?

For example, if you vacuum every night or dust daily and feel you cannot skip a day, your behavior may be compulsive.

If you wash the family towels after one use, ask yourself why. If you must wash dishes after every meal and cannot leave them in the sink or dishwasher, there may be a problem.

Examine your behavior. Think of the time and energy lost doing chores that don't need to be done so often. Take that time and channel it into exercise.

Read each of the chores below, then calculate the time involved each week. Make a decision. Is the chore urgent? Could it be done less often? Check them off accordingly.

How many chores did you consider urgent? _____

Are they really compelling? What would happen if they didn't get done immediately?

List two chores that could be done less often.

_____

_____

Chore	Time (per week)	Urgent?	Could be done less frequently
Laundry	_____	_____	_____
Ironing	_____	_____	_____
Dusting	_____	_____	_____
Vacuuming	_____	_____	_____
Grocery shopping	_____	_____	_____
Dishes	_____	_____	_____
Family shopping	_____	_____	_____
Yard work	_____	_____	_____
Family errands	_____	_____	_____
Correspondence	_____	_____	_____

State how you will decrease the frequency of one of these chores.

How much time could you gain for
exercise every week?

If you didn't check any that could be
done less frequently, think again.
Many mothers have extremely high
standards. Do you need to lower
yours to be more realistic with your
hectic schedule?

Set Priorities

Time for exercise is gained by making chore decisions. You can fix
quicker, smaller, just as nutritious
meals during the week. You can cook
two to three meals when preparing
one and freeze them to save time. You
can dust or vacuum less often. You
might hire someone to come in once a
month for a more thorough cleaning.

You can choose not to iron everything, buy more permanent press
clothes or pay someone to iron for
you. You can do a large grocery shopping once a month, save money for a
dishwasher, tell relatives and friends
that you will be talking to them less
often, turn over errands to family
members. *You don't have to do everything
anymore.*

You can say no more often, resign
from commitments and assign chores
to family members. It is a matter of
priorities.

List one step you can take to gain
time by making a chore decision.

Make Exercise A Family Affair

You have a great opportunity to
model wellness for your children
by exercising. Get them involved. Use
exercise as the family time together.

In the 1980s American children got
fatter and slower. They were found to
have cholesterol problems at a younger and younger age. Today many children have a sedentary lifestyle and are
addicted to television.

Many schools have had to drop
physical education programs because
of budget cuts. It's up to you, if you
possibly can, to encourage your children to get involved in activities and
sports.

Families can exercise together in
many ways. Walking is one of the
healthiest activities and can be a special time together. It's great for your
children. It releases their stress and
tension, thus improving their behavior. It makes them healthier and improves their mood. What more could
you ask? When they are less stressed,
so are you.

Exercising together can be a time
for sharing and catching up with each
other. This can be part of your daily
time with the children.

Loosen up. Get your exercise by
playing with your children. Get a ball
game going, or go to the park and
exercise on the equipment. Play tag
or jump rope. If the weather is bad, go
to the mall and walk. Many schools
have walking programs, too. Make
walking the dog a family affair.

Leisure activities also count. Volleyball, ping-pong, badminton and fris-

bee are healthy. Enroll the family in a YWCA or activity club.

There are dozens of ways for your family to be more active. Some cost money, some are free. Choose what is realistic in terms of time, energy and money. Be creative. Set a family goal. *Any exercise is better than none.*

Do you walk together or exercise as a family?

_____ Yes   _____ No

If no, could you consider this?

_____ Yes   _____ No

List one step you can take to get the entire family more involved in exercise.

_____

_____

How does exercise sound now? Are you enthused? Are you ready for a written guarantee for health and energy? Be creative and realistic in choosing to increase your physical activity.

Don't waste another day of your life being tired. Stop procrastinating and make exercise an "A" priority. You can do it.

Model For Health And Energy

Use exercise for energy

Trade a chore for exercise:
- Switch priorities
- Let something go or do a chore less frequently

Let exercise help you mentally, emotionally and physically:
- Reduce mental stress, release anger and boost self-concept
- Decrease anxiety, panic attacks and depression
- Help weight loss, muscle tone and bone mass
- Prevent heart disease and diabetes

Make exercise a family affair:
- Use physical activity as the family time together
- Exercise to catch up on family communication
- Choose play and leisure activities for exercise

Sneak in exercise:
- Use stairs more
- Walk with co-worker during lunch hour
- Attend exercise program before going home
- Exercise within the home
- Use chores for physical activity

Use exercise to improve your mind, body and emotions to yield health and energy.

9

Get Some Zzzzzs

I fill my energy pool with quality sleep

You spend one third of your lifetime sleeping — or trying to sleep. Sleep is one of the most vital ways that your energy pool is replenished. Yet one out of three mothers, on any given night, struggles to sleep.

Mothers who are short on sleep lose enormous amounts of energy. Chronic fatigue occurs when lack of sleep becomes prolonged and is marked by irritability, lethargy and an insufficient ability to cope. Sleepless mothers can't concentrate, and they live in a state of almost perpetual jet lag.

How much sleep do you need? It's a personal and individual need. Many mothers need seven to eight hours every night. However, a smaller number may need only six hours and others may need up to ten hours.

Pregnancy, stress, grieving, depression and anxiety increase your need for sleep. An occasional missed hour of sleep isn't a problem, but accumulated sleep loss becomes significant.

Sleep provides the energy resources for you to meet the demands of the family . . . the demands of your world. It's also essential for mental alertness. Your sleep schedule plays a key role in keeping your biological rhythms balanced.

Sleep Stealers

From the arrival of the firstborn, most mothers sleep with one ear cocked and one eye opened. This high-alert state continues for the next 20 years. Because women are more sensitive to light and noise, their sleep is disrupted more often than men's.

Insomnia is more common in mothers when the children are preschoolers and when they are teenagers, at different ends of the spectrum. Pleas for a drink of water, bathroom urgencies, lost blankets, teething pain, nightmares or illnesses keep mothers on their toes during the night. Once the driver's license is issued, insomnia returns for obvious reasons.

Stress, depression and anxiety also steal sleep from mothers. Teeth grinding, snoring or restless partners also can keep mothers awake. It's no wonder some mothers are cranky during the day. Quality sleep is necessary . . . yet very few mothers are getting it.

Brief periods of insomnia, occurring from minor stress or traveling, are not a concern. Insomnia lasting for weeks from illness or family strain becomes a problem. Prolonged insomnia, stemming from mental or physical problems, is serious, and professional help may be necessary.

Dietary stimulants and medications for colds, allergies or dieting play their part in keeping mothers awake. Environmental stimuli or vigorous exercise right before bedtime also interferes with needed rest.

Sleep Apnea

Sleep apnea, which stops breathing for up to one minute hundreds of times a night, is serious and needs attention. It affects more males than females and can also be found in children. This condition dramatically affects oxygen levels in the body and can be life-threatening.

Loud snoring and the cessation of breathing occur because muscles of the tongue or back of the throat relax and block the airway. Enlarged tonsils and adenoids can also cause obstruction. Obesity increases this problem. Medical help is needed immediately.

Mothers with apnea wake up exhausted. Excessive daytime sleepiness, morning headaches and confusion are signals. Personality changes can also occur.

The three most common types of insomnia in mothers are: (1) you might struggle to get to sleep; (2) you might wake up or get up with the children throughout the night and have difficulty getting back to sleep; and (3) you might awaken in the early morning such as at 4:00 or 5:00 A.M. Anxiety and anger build as you can't return to sleep before starting your busy day.

How many hours of sleep are you getting at night? _____

Is this enough for you?
_____ Yes _____ No

Are you getting quality sleep?
_____ Yes _____ No

Do you feel rested in the morning?
_____ Yes _____ No

If you answered no to two or three of these questions, you need to evaluate your life. Limit sleep stealers and commit yourself to resolving this sleep problem. Work toward energy restoration.

3 Critical Errors Mothers Make

Mothers who can't sleep at night might be making three critical errors:

1. They don't unwind before bedtime.
2. They overuse substances that stimulate them or interfere with sleep.
3. They throw off their internal clock, disrupting body rhythms.

Some mothers rush about doing all sorts of things right up to the time they collapse in bed exhausted, expecting to fall asleep instantly. Naturally, sleep doesn't come.

Quality sleep requires relaxation. Your mind and body need to unwind for sleep to come. An easing into sleep is necessary.

How much time do you allow to unwind at night? _____

Do you need more time to ease into quality sleep?
_____ Yes _____ No

Mothers often use substances to help them cope during the day that keep them awake at night. Caffeine, which stays in your body up to eight hours, is one of the greatest offenders. Taking in caffeine (in coffee, colas, tea, chocolate or medications) late in the day can keep you awake. Your mind

and body are on speed, unable to relax. Caffeine prevents quality sleep. Make sure your last cup of coffee is six to eight hours before bedtime.

Nicotine from cigarette smoking is a powerful stimulant, too. Smokers have more difficulty falling asleep and experience more fragmented sleep.

Excessive salt/sodium at bedtime may stimulate you. Large amounts of refined sugar products at bedtime swing blood sugar levels during the night, waking you up.

Alcohol disrupts your sleep. You may sleep for a few hours, then feel stimulated. It also suppresses your dream stage of sleep, which is necessary for your mental health.

Do you think that any of these substances prevent you from getting quality sleep? Check appropriate ones.

_____ Caffeine

_____ Nicotine

_____ Excessive salt/sodium

_____ Excessive refined sugar

_____ Alcohol

If you checked one or more offenders, list one step you can take to reduce the problem.

_____

_____

YOUR BIOLOGICAL CLOCK

You sleep, then awaken according to your pre-established biological clock. Your body operates on a 25 to 26 hour cycle, which is run by a clock in your brain. Your mental function, moods, physical performance and biological changes such as temperature fluctuate rhythmically throughout the day and night.

You can help to keep your body clock on target by getting up at approximately the same time every day. On weekends use this time to pamper and nurture yourself. Sip on some herbal tea, take a bath, read a book or watch a tape. Make it your time.

If this internal clock gets off, your sleep/awake cycles are thrown off. Mothers can disrupt this rhythm in several ways.

Disturbed Cycles

If you get up at 5:30 to 6:30 every morning during the week and each Saturday and Sunday sleep until 8:00 or 8:30, your clock is thrown off. By Sunday night you have an accumulated problem.

Combine the disrupted rhythms with Sunday anxieties and the problem heightens. Many mothers suffer anticipatory anxiety Sunday afternoon and evening. They dread starting a new work week, going back to classes or starting the chaotic schedule of child care and school concerns. Monday blues are very common.

Mothers who work the evening or night shift are continuously battling these internal rhythms. You can't always choose your shift, but understanding what is happening helps you cope. Workers are more sluggish and least attentive from 3:00 to 6:00 A.M., increasing the risk of accidents.

Smart supervisors who schedule employees with rotating shifts will move them forward and allow at least three weeks on one shift. For instance, women working the evening shift will be moved to nights, then to days.

Seasonal Affective Disorder

Some mothers, particularly in northern states, may have their internal clocks thrown off in winter by lack of sunlight or decreased light. Seasonal affective disorder (SAD) affects four times more women than men. It causes a recurring winter depression beginning in the fall and lifting in March or April.

Victims of SAD are fatigued, sluggish and have an excessive need for increased sleep. They crave carbohydrates (especially sweets) and experience a weight gain. Mothers perform less efficiently, both mentally and physically, and withdraw socially during this time.

Light therapy (phototherapy), getting outdoors and exercising help many women. Professional help is necessary for moderate or serious depression.

Mothers need to understand these complex body rhythms to learn more about their fluctuating energy levels. If their energy peaks in the morning, they need to do top priority tasks then, when projects can be done more effectively and in less time.

Mothers need to get in touch with their bodies and listen to their inner signals. By understanding their rhythms, they can prevent disruptions to their internal clock and use their energy more efficiently.

Do you get up at approximately the same time seven days a week?

_____ Yes   _____ No

If no, list one step you could take to correct this.

_____

The Three Qs

How can you get quality sleep? Consider the three Qs: Quiet the mind, Quiet the emotions and Quiet the body.

QUIET THE MIND

Allow at least 30 minutes before bedtime for your mind to unwind. Prior to this time, make sure you have completed and prioritized your realistic to-do list for the next day. This helps your mind let go of the day. Deal with your worries and solve your problems early in the evening. Keep paper and pen at your bedside to write down anxieties in the night.

Is your mind racing? Identify why. Adrenaline from stress overload keeps you awake, as does feeling mentally overwhelmed or being on information overload. Anxiety from emotional conflicts or ingesting stimulants can also be a problem.

Diversion and relaxation are now essential. Your mind needs to vegetate. Dim the lights and watch graceful fish swim in an aquarium. Watch a light TV show on PBS with no shouting commercials, or read a boring book.

You might use imagery, letting your mind go to your special place, such as a beach or forest. Meditation helps if it is not too energizing. Teach yourself to relax with calming affirmations, or listen to a relaxation or self-hypnotic tape.

Some mothers use mind games. You might empty out your mind by visualizing the color black. Imagine the back of your forehead as a blackboard. If a worry or anxiety creeps into your mind, write it across the blackboard. Then take an eraser and wipe off the unwanted mental thought. You might bore yourself by reciting the alphabet forward or backward or counting the white fluffy sheep leaping over the fence.

A light carbohydrate snack 30 minutes before bedtime can relax you by releasing calming chemicals in your brain. Air-popped popcorn with minimal salt, rice cakes, bananas, English muffins or a cereal also provide carbohydrates.

Some mothers are helped by a glass of warm milk 30 minutes before bedtime. Eight ounces of milk contain about 300 mg of calcium, which is a natural tranquilizer. It soothes and calms. Chamomile, an herbal tea, is also a relaxant.

Do you write a prioritized to-do list in the early evening?

_____ Yes _____ No

List one step you can take to quiet your mind for better sleep.

_____

_____

QUIET THE EMOTIONS

Release your frustration and anger before bedtime. Make sure conflicts with your children, spouse or significant partner are settled early in the evening.

Let go of anger in constructive ways. Journal writing is one of the best. In the evening write down your thoughts and feelings. Pour out your emotions and unload yourself. Music, deep breathing and relaxation tapes also free pent-up emotions.

List one step you can take to release negative emotions at bedtime.

_____

_____

QUIET THE BODY

Muscular tension constricts blood vessels, preventing necessary blood flow to your brain for good sleep. Release your tension and physical tightness. A bath can soothe you. Turn off your phone and tell family members that you are not to be disturbed.

Make your bath water moderately warm, not hot. A steaming hot bath can be a stimulant and cause your heart to pound.

Enhance the environment. Use candlelight, soft music and fragrances. Aromatic candles, scented beads in a potpourri pot or oils in your bath water aid relaxation. A bath relaxes your muscles and dilates your blood vessels, increasing oxygen flow to your brain.

Muscle tension can also be released by tensing, then relaxing your muscles, one group at a time. Do this in a recliner chair before bedtime or in bed. It is a highly effective way to promote sleep. (Caution: Don't tense muscles in injured or vulnerable areas.)

Relaxation Process

Allow 20 to 30 minutes for this relaxing process. To do this exercise:

1. tense a specific muscle group;
2. hold the tension four to five seconds;
3. release the tension;
4. pause 20 to 30 seconds between each muscle group. During this break, take slow deep breaths, visualizing tension flowing from your body. Let your entire body go limp.

Start with your toes. Flex them up so that they are pointing toward your head. Hold this contraction for four to five seconds. Release the tension. Pause, breathe deeply and relax your entire body.

Move to the next muscle group and repeat the process up your body. Other muscle-group contractions from toe to head include pushing the feet down, pressing the legs into the chair or bed, tightening the buttocks and upper thighs, pulling in the abdominal muscles, arching the back, making fists, pulling both arms to the body, shrugging the shoulders and tensing facial muscles (frown, grimace, tense the jaw, squint the eyes).

Make your own progressive relaxation tape, leading yourself through the four steps with each muscle group. This exercise takes time to learn but its result is priceless.

Deep Breathing

Deep breathing also eases physical tension. Lying in bed at night, relax with several slow, deep breaths. Again, visualize blowing out tension as you exhale. If you wake up in the middle of the night or early morning, refocus on your deep relaxing breaths. Before you know it, you will fall back to sleep.

Mothers with an exercise program sleep better, but avoid aerobic exercise for two hours before bedtime. Vigorous exercise right before bedtime stimulates you and blocks sleep.

Exercise forces physical tension to break up. It also diffuses stress chemicals, which assists sleep.

Eat Lightly

Eat lightly in the evening, and avoid a large meal within four to five hours of bedtime. The reason is simple. You need a good flow of blood to the brain in order to sleep well. A large meal diverts the blood to the stomach to help your digestive process, and sleep is prevented. In addition, a full stomach is uncomfortable and can stimulate stomach acid, which increases heartburn.

Get Tired

Go to bed when your body says it's tired — not before. If you go to bed too early, you will toss and turn and become anxious. If sleep won't come within 30 minutes of going to bed, get up, go to a different room and read or engage in a relaxing activity. Return to bed when you feel drowsy.

Nap Quickly

If you want to nap while the children are napping or in school, make it a short one. A nap of no more than 20 minutes may be energizing, but longer than that sets you up for insomnia that night.

Avoid Sleeping Pills

Don't take medications to sleep. They might backfire and help only temporarily, losing their sleep-inducing property after a week or two. Also they only give you an additional 30 minutes of sleep, yet leave you groggy and sluggish during the day, which you don't need. See a professional, perhaps in a sleep clinic, if your sleep problems are prolonged and serious.

List one step you can take to quiet the body for sleep.

_____

_____

Check Out Your Bedroom

The environment in which you sleep is very important. First, do you have a digital clock near you? The brightness of the dial or the soft clicking sound as the numbers turn over causes insomnia for many mothers.

Move The Clock

Bedside clocks also cause anxiety. Mothers panic when they are up with the children or awake during the night. They count the remaining hours or minutes before morning, which brings more anxiety and makes it almost impossible to return to sleep. This becomes a vicious cycle. Insomnia can be a learned behavior.

Turn your clock away from you. Cover it with a towel or place it on the floor. Resist the temptation to check the time if you are awakened at night.

Although it is hard, retrain yourself. Looking at the clock serves no purpose, but it does escalate anxiety. If you are nervous that the alarm won't go off, set two alarms while you work through this problem.

Check Temperature

Room temperature is also a key factor in sleep quality. A cooler bedroom in the mid-60s may help you sleep better. Allow fresh air in year-round since the air in the house is more polluted than the air outside. In northern states during winter the inside air becomes stagnant. Fresh air with oxygen is needed for good sleep.

Keep It Dark And Quiet

The bedroom should be darkened. This is particularly important for mothers on evening or night shifts who must sleep during the morning and afternoon. Heavy drapes or darkened shades help.

Noise levels need to be considered. Some mothers need complete quiet. Others need the hum of the fan or air conditioner. Music, television, radio and relaxation or environmental tapes are helpful. Ocean waves, bubbling brooks, waterfalls, thunderstorms or crickets ease many mothers into quality sleep.

A Good Bed

Your bed is also important. A good, supportive mattress is key, and your pillow needs to support your head so that your spine and neck are on a straight plane. Do not sleep on your stomach as this causes stressful twisting of your neck vertebrae. Bedclothes and bedcovers need to be light and unrestricting. Make sure you have plenty of space to change positions while you sleep

Check the factors below that you need for better quality sleep.

Ease Your Children Into Slumberland

Mothers can't replenish their energy through quality sleep if the children are up all night. If your children don't sleep, neither will you.

Many children today are also not getting the sleep they need for their health and growth, learning in school and coping with their stress.

Children are getting insufficient sleep for several reasons: (1) Their body rhythms are off because of inconsistent sleep schedules. (2) They are sometimes awakened from a deep sleep early in the morning to be taken to child care. (3) Their increased stress and anxiety levels are causing sleep difficulties. (4) Family changes,

---

_____ Clock turned away

_____ Cool bedroom

_____ Fresh air

_____ Darkened room

_____ Desired noise level

_____ Supportive bed and pillow

_____ Light and unrestricting bedcovers and bedclothes

_____ Plentiful space for changing positions

List one step you can take to change one factor and improve your sleep.

_____

_____

family losses, separation anxiety, teacher conflicts, peer problems and test anxiety are taking their toll.

You can help your children to get better sleep:

- Establish a bedtime ritual. Be consistent with your children, particularly during the work-week, yet remain flexible. Give them a verbal reminder one hour ahead of the approaching bed-time. Use a clock for visual emphasis. Start their ritual activities at this time, such as putting toys away, getting undressed, taking a bath, changing into pajamas, having a bedtime treat and brushing teeth. All of these actions can be part of a nightly ritual.
- Let their minds and bodies relax and prepare for sleep. Allow at least 30 to 40 minutes of quiet time with no stimulation. Dim the lights to induce sleepiness. Limit TV watching. Avoid rough-housing up to one hour before bedtime. Let them listen to soft music or a soothing tape, watch a candle flicker or fish swim or work a puzzle. These are all good pre-bedtime activities.
- Enhance sleep through three powerful actions: (1) a bedtime story or prayer; (2) a positive talk with each child; and (3) touch, such as rocking, cuddling or massage. Always end their day positively by pulling out a special memory. Remind them that tomorrow is a new day.

- Make sure their bedroom is conducive to sleep and put it through the same checklist as yours. A stuffed toy, a special blanket, a nightlight or the door slightly ajar can be reassuring.

When the children are asleep, you can get your needed rest.

List one bedtime ritual you use in your family.

_____

_____

List two unwinding activities your children can use to relax.

_____

_____

_____

_____

Can you improve their bedroom environment for better sleep?

_____ Yes _____ No

If yes, list how.

_____

_____

_____

_____

_____

Quality sleep is essential to your energy. You can fill your energy pool by guaranteeing yourself quality sleep and rest. You can do it.

Model For Health And Energy

Use sleep to replenish your energy pool

Help yourself get quality sleep through Three Qs:
- Quiet the mind
- Quiet the emotions
- Quiet the body

Identify sleep-stealers:
- Stress, anxiety and depression
- Restless bed partners
- Dietary stimulants and drugs
- Environmental stimulation
- Sleep apnea

Assess your sleeping errors:
- No unwinding time
- Overuse of substances that keep you awake
- Disruption of body clock

Get quality sleep and rest to yield health and energy.

Ease your children into slumberland to help your sleep:
- Establish a bedtime ritual
- Let their minds and bodies relax
- Enhance sleep through bedtime stories, positive sharing and cuddling
- Make their bedroom environment conducive to sleep

10

Conquer The Battle Over Chores

*I promote family teamwork for
chores to save my energy*

When you were pregnant the first time, you dreamed of a family working together . . . total peace . . . total harmony. Today your dream has faded away. In reality you struggle for a better way to share chores.

Battles over chores rip a family apart faster than any other threat. Domestic tasks cause bickering, fighting, stalling and outright refusal. These conflicts drain away a mother's energy. Nothing challenges a family more than confrontations over chores.

But chores don't have to be a bone of contention. Each family defines what is important to them. Values need to be clarified, and decisions on who will do what tasks involve all family members, regardless of age.

Chores Teach Children

Chores are powerful, lifetime learning tools. They develop valuable skills and build character. (See Figure 10.1)

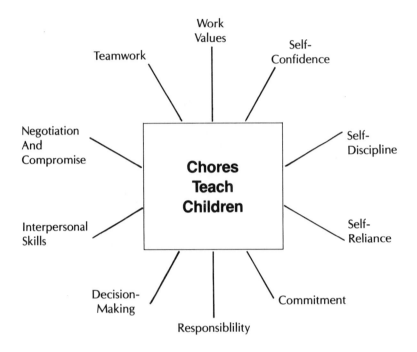

Figure 10.1. Chores Teach Children

Develop Values

Children develop work values when they are involved in tasks early in their lives. They learn that work is a necessary ingredient in life. They find that this work ethic brings compensations, sometimes financial. Other gains are equally important.

Psychological Gains

Their self-esteem soars as they accomplish tasks and learn skills. They feel important, accepted and part of a group. This esteem bolsters their self-confidence.

Self-discipline and self-reliance are additional gains. Children learn commitment and responsibility, which help develop self-control. Their semi-independence in doing chores enhances their decision-making ability and sense of autonomy. These traits build confidence.

Interpersonal Skills

Interpersonal skills develop as families work with chores. Children learn to communicate, listen, negotiate and compromise. Positive confrontation can be practiced. They master give and take.

Most importantly, chores teach teamwork. Team-building skills are valuable in later careers and adult relationships, which are highly affected by family experiences.

Family Teamwork Reduces Stress

Family teamwork is life-giving to a mother. It reduces her stress and helps her pace her energy, preventing depletion of her resources.

Are your family members working as a team regarding chores?

_____ Yes _____ No

If yes, list two qualities or skills that your children are learning through their chores.

_____

_____

If no, would you like your family to handle chores differently?

_____ Yes _____ No

Are You Blocking Teamwork?

Mothers don't mean to sabotage chores, it just happens. You might be a compulsive perfectionist and prefer to do the tasks yourself or redo them so that everything is just the way you want it to be.

You swirl around remaking beds and reloading the dishwasher. You dust over their efforts and vacuum areas they missed, believing you are teaching them what's right.

You tell your family: "You tried, but it's not quite good enough. I'll take care of it." Family members begin to think, "Why bother. I can't do anything to please her." These messages often go unsaid.

Or you might be a martyr. Because of low self-esteem or guilt, you feel you deserve to be used and stepped on. You therefore hold back from asking for help and assigning chores to family members. You do it all and anger and resentment build.

Or you may have an obsessive need to be everything to everybody, a people pleaser. Filling your needs by handling all of the chores hurts your family. These behaviors block family teamwork.

Mothers who protect their children from chores do them a grave injustice. These youngsters can grow up to be irresponsible and to be takers in society. Their adult relationships fail because they haven't learned how to work together.

Avoid The Destructive Nagging Cycle

Are you a hurried mother? Do you start chores in anger because family members aren't moving fast enough? Do you nag to no avail? Do you feel unheard? Does your rage seethe?

Does your spouse or partner drag his feet? Do you waste your time nagging? Does he fail to sense your urgency?

Most men do not like to be told what to do. They resist orders. You nag, nag, nag; he stalls, stalls, stalls. You threaten . . . nothing gets done. There are no winners.

Give him a day or two to get a couple of chores done. This might work. Give him a 15-minute deadline, and tasks won't even get started. Because part of the problem concerns control, you might as well save your energy.

Don't force your standards on your family. Most chores don't have to be done right away. You are not always right — they are not always wrong.

Seek Compromise

Recognize the potpourri of different personalities in your family. You may have manipulators, rebels, bosses or pleasers. Appreciate them all for their uniqueness. Your family members have different values and different ways of doing things. Go for a compromise.

Permit a child's bedroom to be straightened and semiorganized. Don't push for perfection. Some of the world's greatest slobs grow up to excel in neatness.

Ask your spouse or children for a reasonable time limit to do a job. Put them in the driver's seat. Don't impose your time urgency. Let go.

Assess Your Contribution

Mothers don't set out to sabotage chores, but their personality quirks dampen getting the job done. Look at your own traits and behaviors, and determine if they are indeed blocking teamwork in your family.

Do you redo the children's chores to have things done "just right"?
_____ Yes _____ No

Do you end up doing tasks because you do them faster?
_____ Yes _____ No

Do you struggle asking family members to help?
_____ Yes _____ No

Are you inconsistent in following up on the children's chores because you feel guilty?
_____ Yes _____ No

List one step you can take to improve family teamwork by changing your expectations.

Build A Family Team For Sharing Chores

Make a firm commitment that you are going to eliminate these chore battles. Involve every family member. Your energy and health are at stake. You do not have to do it all.

1. HOLD A THINK-TANK SESSION

Call a major family conference, and explain that you need their help. How can chores get done? How can the home run more smoothly? How can there be less conflict in this area to save everyone's energy?

Brainstorm with family members: Name every chore that is necessary to run a household. Write them down. Use a participatory approach, and encourage everyone to contribute to the list. View all family members as equal and capable of good ideas. Cooperation is the goal.

Bite your lip and stay open to everyone's input. Regardless of age or gender, regardless of right or wrong, respect their ideas. See what you can learn from them. Make every idea important.

2. PUT CHORES INTO CATEGORIES

Food:
Meal planning
Grocery shopping
Cooking

Meal cleanup
Dishes

Domestic:
Laundry
Folding clothes
Ironing
Dusting
Vacuuming
Washing mirrors
Scrubbing floors
Cleaning bathroom(s)

Miscellaneous Inside:
Plant care
Pet care
Paying bills
Balancing checkbook
Fall/spring cleaning
Telephoning
Family correspondence
Social engagements
Cleaning basement

Child care: (Younger child)
Feeding
Bathing
Dressing
Supervising

Overseeing: (School-age child)
Lunches
Packing for school
Homework
Chauffeuring

Outside:
Recycling
Garbage
House maintenance
Washing windows
Cleaning garage
Trimming shrubs
Gardening
Raking leaves
Shoveling snow
Mowing lawn

3. SIMPLIFY THE CHORE LIST

You might concentrate only on the tasks that need to be done weekly. Such tasks as family correspondence, cleaning the basement or washing mirrors can be delayed in stressful times. Spring and fall cleaning are rarely done today. There are no serious consequences if these are missed.

A written chore list is a learning tool. It offers a visual record of family needs and validates the huge number of tasks that go into running a home.

4. EMPHASIZE "WE ARE A TEAM"

Every person living under your roof — regardless of gender or age — is part of a team. All family members need to be active players if goals are to be achieved.

Use the analogy of a baseball team. Every member on a team is involved in practice and games and is expected to contribute to the team success in many ways. Winning a baseball game depends on group participation. So does running your home.

Kids Can Participate

Preschoolers can help immensely. Even a toddler can help pick up toys, carry a plastic cup to the sink, help you make a bed or throw small items into the dryer.

Children, by ages three to five, are good helpers. They can help clean their rooms and do many other tasks, such as helping with food preparation, setting the table, recycling, dusting low furniture and loading the dishwasher. Get your children involved in family responsibilities when they are young.

Younger children need help with chores. You need to guide them and provide direction, but make it a game. For instance, using a timer works well with this age group.

School-age children between five and ten can pitch in and work more independently. In addition to the above tasks, they can graduate to pet and plant care, making beds, vacuuming, dishes, taking out the garbage and putting away groceries. Somewhere between eight and ten, they can start doing laundry chores.

From eleven on, the sky's the limit, depending on age and maturity. But remember, your children are also more involved in school projects and extracurricular activities and also have more homework. Eventually as they get jobs, time becomes a problem for them, too. Don't overload them.

Your preteen and teenager can assume more responsible tasks, such as doing the laundry, ironing and outside chores.

Get them involved early in grocery shopping. Teach them the value of money, reading labels, using coupons and getting sale items. Once they get their driver's license, they can take over the grocery shopping. Give them the space to learn, allowing for mistakes.

5. LET FAMILY MEMBERS DIVIDE CHORES

Step back as a mother and let the children take over the division of chores. Tell them you want three to five ideas. Remind them that tasks need to fit the age of the child. Give them ownership in this process. Re-member, you also want to teach cooperation and participation.

Hold a family vote once their plan is complete. When your family members define the who, what, where, when and why, the probability of cooperation and success increases.

Here are sample ideas of dividing chores:

- *Volunteer approach.* Let them define how much they will help. This approach can have problems in fairness.
- *Sign-up sheet.* Post the list and allow them to sign up for the three tasks they want. The first to choose gets the best selections, so make sure the chores are age appropriate.
- *Rotate.* Alternate chores weekly or biweekly.
- *Chore toss.* Write responsibilities on pieces of paper, which are folded and placed in a container. Call a family meeting and toss the chores up in the air. Each member grabs three or four chores.
- *Task draw.* Put written tasks in a shoebox or bowl. Let family members draw out three or four.
- *Chore vacation.* Rotate chores among family members, with each person getting a week off from chores every six weeks.

6. PROVIDE OPTIONS AND FLEXIBILITY

Turning over chores yields greater cooperation. Let family members trade chores if it is agreeable to both parties and they are near the same age. Older children should not be allowed to switch a hard chore for an easy one with a young child.

Let them barter. If a child wants to exchange a lighter load one week for a heavier load the next with a sibling, stay out of the bargaining. This helps them with negotiating skills. Fairness and getting the tasks done are the goals.

Remain flexible with time. Pushing time urgency causes resistance. Give them hours or a day or two to complete a job. This helps them develop responsibility, self-discipline and decision-making. You might say in the morning, "Let's rent some videos tonight and make popcorn. Let's have all of our chores done by 7:00. Okay?" Get their commitment.

7. DELEGATE

Delegate chores only as a last resort. However, if all efforts to make them responsible fail, it might be necessary.

Delegating has problems. It does not teach team effort, and it is authoritarian and says, "I'll tell you what to do and I expect it to be obeyed."

It is insensitive to the feelings of family members. It does not yield compliance or produce cooperation. Instead, it provokes resistance and conflicts with today's team approach for smoother family functioning.

List one way by which chores are now divided in your family.

Write one step you can take to divide chores more equally.

The A-P Approach Works

A = Acknowledge! P = Praise! Recognize your children's help by giving them positive feedback. Every human being needs affirmation. You do, too. Although your children need to develop their own internal motivation, external support is essential.

"Catch" them in positive behaviors that often go unnoticed. Unintentionally many mothers focus on the negative things their children do. The positives need more attention. Children of all ages excel with recognition.

Let your praise be coaching and encouraging. Cultivate the idea of family teamwork. Guide them in learning how to be a team player.

Praise can be overdone, however, and excessive praise is counterproductive. Don't be flowery or sugary. Children know when you're overdoing it.

Appreciation can be expressed in small ways. Smile. Say, "Thank you for vacuuming. It looks better, doesn't it?" Hugs are great incentives. Hang a chore board that displays stars or stickers to reinforce and praise chore completion publicly.

Payment For Chores

Should you pay for chores done? Probably not. This reimbursement detracts from the goals of teaching teamwork, life skills and self-esteem. Remember also that every member living under your roof contributes to maintaining their home. Payment confuses this commitment and conveys the wrong message.

Money for extra chores is more appropriate for teenagers. You might hire your teen to do additional tasks. You need the help, the teen needs the money. This works well.

Families are healthier and happier when all members pitch in. Energy is more abundant, and stress levels and interpersonal conflicts are greatly reduced.

List one way you can affirm family cooperation.

_____

_____

Consequences For Nonparticipation

As your children grow, their lives become more complex, and at times they won't want to be team players. They get overworked and tired. Make sure your children aren't rebelling because they are on overload.

If cooperative children suddenly turn uncooperative, give them the benefit of the doubt, and try to get to the bottom of their changed behavior. Are they troubled? Stressed out? Having peer problems in school or in conflict with a teacher? Is your family having increased problems?

Take them shopping, out to eat or for a ride. Get them away from home and siblings. Share your concerns over their changed behavior. Ask them to share why they are dragging their feet with chores. Listen. Hear

their thoughts and feelings. Acknowledge their sharing.

If your children are going through a hard time, ease up temporarily. Agree on a time when they will resume doing chores. However, if it is just a phase they are going through, reiterate the importance of family cooperation.

If you're seriously concerned about a child's refusal to do chores, you can best resolve the problem through a participatory approach. Allow older offenders to list possible consequences.

Realistic Consequences

What consequences are realistic? Will you restrict an allowance, TV use or having friends over? For drivers, will car privileges or extracurricular activities be on the line? How long should the consequences last?

Review their ideas. Your children might be harder on themselves than you would be. Negotiate with them. When possible, use one of their solutions to reach a compromise. Consequences need to match the age of your children.

Contract writing is powerful with teenagers. Let your teenager draw up the agreement. Make sure the consequences and time limits are clear. Have all involved parties sign it. Written commitments are more forceful than verbal agreements.

Children need to learn early on that there are consequences for the decisions they make, that there are outcomes for their choices. Chores are no different.

GET PARTNERS TO COOPERATE

A spouse or significant partner can either make or break family cooperation. More men are helping within the home, yet the number is still too low. The distribution of chores remains highly unequal.

If the male in your life is pitching in with home responsibilities, he is helping you protect your energy. On the other hand, if he believes that chores are not his problem, he can cause you prolonged energy drain. Men who refuse to help with chores cause tremendous stress within the family.

If there is a problem, address this with the man in your life. Make a date away from home, and go out to eat and share this pressing conflict. Males have been groomed to be problem-solvers. Ask him to come up with several solutions, and respect his input. Do some negotiating, using his ideas if possible. Make him part of the solution. You may reach a compromise on how he can help more.

Conflicts in this area can cause such strain and energy drain that professional help may be necessary. A mediator, couple's support group or family counseling is often needed. If all this fails, you still have a few choices.

You can lower your domestic standards dramatically and stop doing for everyone. This isn't easy, but it may be needed. Martyrdom is out.

List one step you can take to clarify consequences for non-cooperative family members.

_____

_____

_____

_____

Declaration Of War

You have been nice (sometimes too nice). You have hinted you need help — to no avail. You have sat back and watched, but no one did anything. You have asked, pleaded and threatened. You are at your wit's end. War needs to be declared.

STOP DOING

Just stop doing for everyone. Dirty clothes stay on the floor. Towels stay in a heap. Washed clothes stay in the dryer. You don't iron. This is the fastest way to get attention. This is the best way to be heard. Call an all-out strike.

Do you need to go on strike now? _____ Yes _____ No

How To Call A Strike

There is a right and a wrong way to call a strike. Don't scream "STRIKE!" in a fit of rage. This type of resistance will be short-lived. Your family won't take you seriously, and in fact they will find this funny. A successful strike follows a strategic process. Consider these steps:

ANALYZE

Study the problem, and write down the reasons why the strike is necessary. Are your motives valid? What main objective do you hope to achieve. Is this strike a last resort? Has everything else been tried by now?

DESIGN A STRATEGY

Plan every step of the attack. When will the strike take place? Set a date. What publicity do you need to do ahead of time? List what you need to do to prepare. How intensively will you picket? What number of responsibilities will you let go — to what extent? How long will you stay on strike? What will you do if the strike backfires?

PREPARE THE PUBLICITY

You will want to wear a sign at home that reads "Mom on strike — Do not disturb." You will want eight to ten banners to put throughout the house, on the refrigerator, across the washer and on the television to remind your family that you are serious. You might want to put a picket sign in the front yard that reads "Mom on strike." If you want to make an impact — make a good impact. Now the sneak attack is ready.

CALL A FAMILY SUMMIT

The time has arrived. Call the troops together and announce the strike. Keep your cool. Be specific and state your facts. Tell them the length of the strike. Define what activities are stopping.

"I am going on strike for one week."
"You are on your own."

"I am not preparing any meals."
"I am not doing laundry."
"There is no taxi cab."
Repeat the stopped activities, and post a written list. Despite pleas, stick to your guns. Hold the fort.

Curl up in a recliner chair with your favorite novel. Imagine having an entire week off from family demands. If anyone approaches you for a favor, calmly reinforce that you are on strike. Not available.

It's too bad that mothers have to get to this stage, but strikes *are* highly effective.

By the third day of the strike, family members may be ready to negotiate. Be cautious and go slowly. Make sure that they are serious and ready to cooperate. Has enough time passed so that this event will never be forgotten?

Get It In Writing

If a peace treaty is timely, insist that everything be in writing. Let them draw up the contract for negotiations. Read it carefully before signing. Teamwork should resume.

Chores are a family affair. Everyone under your roof is part of a team. Stop feeling responsible for policing chores and give up some control. Turn your power over to other family members. Let cooperation be their idea.

Your energy is being drained by their resistance to pitch in. You can't afford it. And neither can they.

Model For Health And Energy

Let chores teach
children:
- Work values
- Self-esteem
- Self-reliance
- Interpersonal skills
- Teamwork

Acknowledge and praise:
- Catch your children in
  positive behaviors
- Teach and encourage
  them

Don't sabotage chore
teamwork:
- Decrease compulsiveness
- Respect differing
  standards
- Accept a good job
- Let family members
  define time limits

Define consequences for
uncooperative family
members:
- Investigate chore refusal
- Let family members list
  consequences
- Negotiate and
  compromise
- Declare war and call
  a strike

Build a family team
for chores:
- Hold a think-tank
  session
- Categorize chores, then
  simplify the list
- Emphasize:
  "We are a team"
- Let family members
  divide chores
- Provide options and
  flexibility

Use teamwork in family
chores to yield health and
energy.

11

Mothers Who Laugh
— Last!

*I laugh for energy and to
keep my perspective on life*

Think about your childhood. Remember the nonstop giggles with your best friend? Did you ever get into trouble for inappropriately giggling during a solemn occasion — giving a speech, attending a funeral or singing in a church choir? Were you ever sent to the principal's office because of inappropriate laughter?

You were born with a sense of humor that developed in your early years. When you were a little girl, smiling and laughing may have come easily. Humor may have been second nature.

If your childhood was traumatic, humor may have been lost along the way. Dysfunctional families stifle humor and playfulness.

How is your sense of humor now — alive and well, or buried somewhere between childhood and adulthood?

As a mother you may be so intense that you forget you have a sense of humor. Your life might be clouded with seriousness, and you may find it impossible to lighten up and enjoy the energizing qualities of humor and laughter.

If you have suppressed your sense of humor, you are missing out on needed health and energy. This loss is affecting your family too.

Have You Lost It?

Have you lost your sense of humor? Find out to what extent you need to be rejuvenated. Read each statement, and score yourself:

1. no
2. sometimes
3. yes

_____ Family members would agree that I have a good sense of humor.

_____ I can laugh at myself.

_____ As a family we act silly at times.

_____ I feel energized by laughter.

_____ My family watches humorous shows or rents funny videos.

_____ I pull on my sense of humor when I am stressed out.

_____ As a family we share funny situations.

_____ I use humor and laughter to keep a perspective on life.

_____ Family members post cartoons or comic strips around our house.

_____ I believe humor is a survival skill in today's world.

Score: If you scored under 15, you might be humor-impaired. Think about how you might increase your sense of humor. If you scored 15 to 24, you are on your way to appreciating humor power. If you scored 25 to 30, congratulations. Your family is very lucky.

If you scored poorly on this inventory, there is hope. Learn about the energy and health behind humor. Rediscover your playful inner child.

One thing I learned from taking the humor test is _____

_____

_____

Building A Case For Lightness

Mothers today are on the run. They are tired and need quick and continued energy. Laughter offers instant energy . . . humor provides sustained energy.

Being a mother is serious business. But humor is a priceless commodity that helps your family survive in a challenging world and prevents you from becoming too intense. Humor and laughter force you to keep your perspective on life's happenings and offer you balance.

Picture yourself on a high wire, teetering along, trying to balance all of your roles. Visualize humor as an equalizer, steadying you, preventing you from tumbling and falling apart.

Humor is healthy when it does not compromise another human being. Humor can be gentle; humor can be subtle. Laughing with, not at, others is the key.

Laughter breaks up your day. It intercepts your rapid pace by slowing down your treadmill and compelling you to pause for a moment to re-energize. It is healthy and badly needed for mothers, yet is too rarely enjoyed.

I need more humor and laughter in my life.

_____ Yes _____ No

My family needs to lighten up.

_____ Yes _____ No

If you answered yes to both questions, make a serious commitment to lighten up in small steps.

Mental, Emotional And Physical Effects Of Laughter

For centuries humor has been used to boost moods and help healing. In the 13th century it helped to speed healing after minor surgery. Hundreds of years later it was used to treat melancholy.

Serious research has been conducted on humor for the past 30 years. Laughter was found to provide a healthy workout to the face, chest and abdomen. Robust laughter gave the internal organs a vigorous workout. Organs were literally massaged during laughter. Belly laughter was dubbed "internal jogging." Other studies found that laughter decreased pain and improved the immune system.

LAUGH THERAPY

Today humor is used increasingly in health facilities — hospitals and nursing homes. Humor is viewed as therapeutic along with medical intervention. Laughter works preventively — it provides health maintenance. A laugh a day may keep the doctor away.

Laughter is life-giving and boosts your energy reserves. When you laugh, especially a deep belly laugh, you exercise your lungs. (See Figure 11.1)

Laughter forces stagnant air out of your lungs. It increases your oxygen intake. This is very important for mothers, for whom more oxygen means more energy. The oxygen travels via the bloodstream to your brain and muscles. You are mentally and physically energized, improving your overall function.

Laughter also energizes you by relieving stress and tension. Laughter slows the release of stress chemicals. Through a hearty laugh, mental, emotional and physical stress are released. Since laughing is a workout, it dissipates your stress chemicals.

Laughing forces your tense muscles to relax through a series of muscular contractions and releases. You cannot laugh and stay rigidly tense — it's impossible.

Laughter changes your brain chemistry, impacting your mental, emotional and physical health. Laughing provides a quick mental diversion — a respite from worry and gloomy thoughts. It intercepts your seriousness . . . it clarifies your thinking. Laughing offers stress resiliency, making you better able to face life's adversities. It may even prolong your life.

Emotional Benefits

Emotionally, laughter counteracts fear, anger and depression. It puts life into perspective, thus alleviating fears. It diffuses pent-up anger and rage and lifts you up when you are down. It prevents hardening of the attitudes.

Brain chemicals are triggered by laughter. The endorphins make you feel good. They put you in a state of euphoria . . . a sense of well-being. The catecholamines may help to reduce inflammation from arthritis and relieve pain.

Think of the power and energy you could have for just a few laughs a day. Do you laugh at least ten times a day? Are four of those laughs deep, belly laughs?

When is the last time you laughed, really laughed?

_____

_____

What made you laugh?

_____

_____

How many times a day do you enjoy a good laugh?

_____

_____

Do you think you laugh enough?

_____

_____

Getting Up When You're Down — 4 Secrets

Would you like to be less serious, happier, less intense and more vivacious? Would you like to have more energy and be in a better mood more of the time? You can do it.

1. GET IN TOUCH WITH THE HUMOR AROUND YOU

Look around. Humor surrounds you everywhere. You may miss it all because you are too busy — too busy to even capture playful moments with your family. You may be caught in the fast lane that traps so many of today's mothers. No wonder you are tired.

Pause for a moment. Watch toddlers; they're great teachers in the joy of living. Focus on how they respond to their environment. Study the way they catch and enjoy the moment, smiling at the simple things in life: chasing a butterfly, following a caterpillar or toddling after a rolling ball.

When was the last time you stopped to enjoy a light moment? How long has it been since you sat and enjoyed nature, smelled flowers or shared a hilarious situation with your family? Is it overdue? Why?

2. LIVE IN THE PRESENT

Make a commitment to pause periodically throughout the day and enjoy the moment. Determine to get more lightness in your life. Try simple changes.

You might try to smile more frequently. Even if you are down or in a lousy mood, force a smile. The muscles used in a broad smile can increase blood flow to your brain, making you feel better. Smiling changes moods.

Surprise family members. Greet them in the morning with a big smile. Smiles are contagious . . . one size

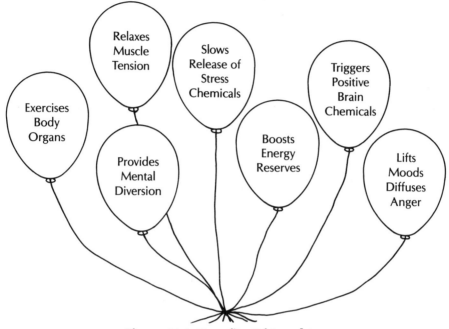

Figure 11.1. Benefits Of Laughter

fits all. Perhaps your smile will rub off, and everyone will be in a better mood.

Share a little humor. Use humorous stationery or postcards for correspondence. If friends are ill, get them a humorous book instead of flowers. You might make your own funny greeting card, buy joke gifts or wrap up old household items for celebrations. You might start wearing humorous T-shirts or sweatshirts.

3. ENJOY HUMOROUS ACTIVITIES

Watch a light TV program or attend a comedy club. Go to a performance of a humorous play. Read contemporary greeting cards at stores or browse through rows of humorous

books in bookstores. Subscribe to humorous magazines. Rent videos of funny films.

Enjoy your favorite comic strips every day. Be on the lookout for cartoons in professional journals or family magazines. Create a "funny" file of miscellaneous items that evoke humor and laughter, and reread the collection if you are down.

4. PULL ON YOUR SUPPORT SYSTEM

Surround yourself with fun people. Evaluate the relationships in your life, and determine if some are blocking your humor and laughter.

If you are down, touch base with a good friend who appreciates humor.

Go out and share a light conversation or a humorous situation at home or work. Talk about positive happenings or happy memories.

It's easy to get down in today's world, so don't let yourself. Limit the pity parties to 15 minutes. Be on the alert to catch yourself heading toward a bad mood and take action. There are many ways to rise above the downs of today.

You can rejuvenate yourself. You are creative and ingenious. Reach out for the simple things in life . . . a little fun, a little play, lighter talk and humorous sharing topped with a few laughs.

List one thing you can do to lift yourself up when you are down.

_____

_____

4 Ways To Bond The Family With Humor

Humor and laughter are electrifying forces that spark life in the family, stimulating and motivating its members.

Humor is a connector, bringing family members together and, like an adhesive, holding them together during the hard times. It is a stabilizer that cements the family together against outside adversities.

Family relationships are strengthened by humor and laughter. Cooperation is improved, family goals are reached more quickly, and family stress and tension are diffused and lowered when humor is part of the picture.

Some mothers feel that if they promote humor within the family, they will not be respected. They fear losing their authoritative image. It's quite the opposite.

You are much more credible to your family if you lighten up and admit you are human. You will gain more respect by using these potent skills — humor and laughter. Don't be afraid of making yourself vulnerable.

Cultivate a sense of humor in your home to bond the family. Humor, laughter and playfulness offer a balance for families caught up in a tension-filled world.

1. COACH FAMILY HUMOR

You can promote humor in the home in several ways. First, model humor yourself. Learn to laugh at yourself. Humor and laughter are contagious, and family members will catch on rapidly.

Humor is the great communicator. Take advantage of this. Humor boosts sharing and puts family members in touch with each other. Use humor to help family members express themselves, release creativity for problem-solving and improve overall communication.

Humor sharpens listening skills. Your messages, injected with lightness, are heard, not lost. Requests topped with humor are more powerful than nagging and begging.

You might, for instance, say to your teenager, "The garbage truck moves into your bedroom at 5:00 tomorrow. Everything not on shelves or in your closet will be removed. Good luck." Keep your word. Family members get the message.

Use bedtime to encourage humor. Teach your children to end their day on a light, positive note. As you tuck your children into bed at night ask them to share the funniest thing that happened that day.

2. PLASTER FAMILY HUMOR AROUND

Reach out and touch someone. Use verbal and visual reminders of humor throughout the house and outside, too. Encourage the posting of cartoons or comic strips on the refrigerator or central communication board. You might assign the search for amusing funnies as a weekly chore to be rotated among family members. Try using humor magnets on your refrigerator.

Funny signs, posters or books throughout the home can also spread humor. You might make a family scrapbook of funny family pictures, jokes or magazine cut-outs. You might have a stuffed animal as a family mascot. Give the mascot to family members when they are down. Spread some lightness.

Stretch humor around through communication. Foster the sharing of knock-knock jokes or funny situations. You might create a pass-along story. One family member starts the story, then other members build on it. Send funny love notes in your children's lunch boxes.

You might write some Murphy Laws as a family. At night you could turn out the lights and create funny stories.

You might use pet names or nicknames with family members. Allow for healthy teasing that does not offend family members. Let your children play occasional practical jokes on you. Try to find humor in minor disasters.

You might tape family members laughing and having a good time. If you notice moods are down, play the tape and watch the wondrous change.

Go to the library and check out comedy cassettes or videos as a family. Make your own family video of treasured moments.

3. CAPTURE PLAYFULNESS

Mothers need to play more often. It might only be for 15 minutes a day, but it is essential for your survival. Playfulness boosts balance, energy and self-confidence in the family.

Pause more frequently to capture the moment. Chances are that, at any given moment, something humorous is brewing around you. Become more aware. Watch your pets — the cat chasing its tail or pouncing on a movement of the waterbed, your dog and child playing together with a ball.

Make chores more fun. Let your children give you creative ideas. You might get bright-colored dust cloths or dye the mop a bright color. Do chores to the family's favorite music.

Play more games together. Pictionary Jr., Pit, Monopoly or Scrabble promote family dynamics. Outside, play more games like hide-and-seek, statue and tag.

Rake leaves or shovel snow as a family, taking the time to jump into the leaves or the snowbank. Build a snowman and make it look funny.

Music is a natural for triggering playfulness. Enjoy a family sing-a-long. Get rhythm band instruments for members to play along. Music is powerful in altering moods, so use it often.

Create your own family playfulness. Enjoy an occasional pillow fight. Outside, experience a water-pistol fight or fill balloons with water and hold a balloon-popping contest. Run through the sprinkler.

Enjoy sports. Light wrestling, playful boxing, badminton and volleyball can be fun.

Your community can offer resources for playfulness. Plan family trips to the zoo, park or beach. Look for a bargain at a hotel, and take the family on an overnight surprise to enjoy the swimming and fun activities.

4. ESTABLISH FUN TRADITIONS

On holidays plan special picnics or get-togethers with relatives or neighbors. Have a barbecue and play games (e.g., softball or volleyball). Create a play, hold a gong show or play charades.

Once a month have a reverse dinner. Start the meal with a healthy dessert, then work backward to the salad or appetizer. Let the children plan and make it.

There are dozens of ways to inject more humor in your family life. Start with a few ideas.

State one way you could spread humor around your home.

_____

_____

List two ways you could increase your playfulness as a mother.

_____

_____

_____

State one fun tradition you have as a family.

_____

_____

You have a serious job to do as a mother, but you can use humor along the way. Life is too short to spend it being somber. Humor and laughter are not meant to replace the realities of today's challenges or to be a cure-all, but they can help you survive as a mother.

Model For Health And Energy

Assess if you have lost your
sense of humor

Get yourself up when you're
down:
- Look at humor
  around you
- Bring past humor to
  present
- Enjoy humorous media
  and activities
- Surround yourself with
  fun people

Use humor and
laughter for:
- Energy
- Balance in your life
- Health

Laughter benefits:
- Provide "internal
  jogging"
- Decrease pain
- Boost the immune
  system
- Increase oxygen for
  energy
- Relieve stress and
  tension
- Change brain chemistry
  for better functioning
  and well-being

Bond the family with
humor:
- Coach family humor
- Plaster humor around
- Capture playfulness
- Establish fun traditions

Increase humor and
laughter to yield health
and energy.

12

Mothers On The Double Shift

*I pace myself at work
for energy on the second shift*

First shift: economic necessity. Second shift: family necessity. Can you do it? You may have pangs of doubt, pangs of guilt. Is it possible for you to balance your first and second shifts?

It is if you conserve your energy and pace yourself for survival. Both shifts need to be covered. Ration out your energy on the first shift. You need to function at home as well as at work. You can't be there for the second shift if the first shift has totally drained you. You and your family are going to suffer.

Mothers have a full-time job within the home. Many also work outside the home because their earnings today have become necessary, not supplementary. Money is especially critical to the many households headed by women. It's called survival.

Today more than half of all women with children younger than six work outside the home. Over three-fourths of American women with children six to 16 work outside the home, whether part time or full time. Energy resources are the key to making it all work.

Three factors help mothers pace their energy on the first shift:

- Quality child care
- A healthy work environment
- Safety valves at work (see Chapter 13)

Do you have these positive elements in your life?

_____ Yes   _____ No

The Child-Care Crisis

Shockingly, the United States lags behind most industrialized countries in family-support policies. Mothers, children and families must become a government priority.

American organizations offering child-care assistance are few. Employers are attempting to increase on-site or near-site child-care programs.

"Family friendly" companies are increasing, but not fast enough. Their positive support is paying off with reduced absenteeism, increased productivity, less workplace stress and decreased employee turnover.

What do you want as a mother working outside the home? Beyond good and safe child care and after-school programs, mothers want options. They want alternatives, such as flexible scheduling, job sharing, part time versus full time and family leave with job protection. Other wishful benefits include a sympathetic supervisor, opportunities to complete work at home and referral services for unexpected emergencies.

The cost of good child care nationwide is escalating. For this reason, some mothers are resigning from full-time positions and are choosing part-time work, staying at home or starting innovative home businesses.

For single mothers heading households, it is not so easy, with two additional factors compounding the difficulty. First, women continue to fall behind men in pay received for full-time comparable work. Second, financial support from some fathers remains unpredictable or nonexistent. Some legislation has been enacted to curb this neglect, but enforcement has been weak.

A changing culture and society also alter child-care assistance. Extended family support may be minimal because families are mobile, and grandparents might live in other states. Even if grandparents are in the area, they are often in the workforce themselves.

Mothers are more focused and productive workers when they know their children are safe and secure. In contrast, mothers who worry constantly about their children are distracted and struggle to be productive. They are anxious, and anxieties cause stress and drain energy resources. Everyone loses.

Take Action For Change

How can you get quality care? Talk to other families. Discuss child-care options in community settings, such as PTA meetings, religious activities, health-care agencies or support groups. Review facilities listed in newspapers.

Exchange information with mothers who work with you. Where are their children? Why? It may be difficult to find someone to come into your home, but family day care is increasingly available, and child-care programs are offered by many community services.

List one positive feature about your present child-care arrangement.

_____

_____

Write down one thing you would like to change.

_____

_____

How does your workplace support you as a mother?

_____

_____

Child-Care Checklist

You have a right to certain child-care expectations, no matter what care you choose. If you have children in a program now, use the checklist to evaluate their current care. The following questions center on safety, physical and psychological health and compatibility with your values.

Check each factor you have investigated.

_____ Is the center close to home and work?

_____ Is the child-care setting licensed or registered with the state or another agency? Regulation varies from state to state.

_____ Have you interviewed the director and staff and visited the setting during challenging times, when, for example, children may be tired?

_____ What credentials do the providers have? Do they have a child development background? Are they sensitive to the children and encourage them? Do the children seem content?

_____ What's the ratio of providers to children? Infants and toddlers need more providers. Compare ratios with other centers.

_____ Are activities structured as well as offering spontaneity? Are toys safe and appropriate for various ages?

_____ Are healthy snacks, meals and rest periods provided?

_____ Is there a staff member with CPR and first-aid training?

_____ Does the environment have fire extinguishers and smoke alarms? Are other safety factors in place?

_____ Does the center have good ventilation?

_____ How is discipline handled by the caregivers? Are rules and limits made clear to the children and parents? Are problems discussed with the parents?

_____ Are child-care policies regarding fees, hours, sickness and accidents in writing?

_____ Can you get names of other parents as references?

List two child-care factors that you consider most important.

_____

_____

List one step you can take to secure good child care.

_____

_____

School-Age Children

What about school-age children? Their care is equally important and creates greater anxiety because thousands of latchkey children return to empty houses every day. Most companies do not provide assistance, and schools and community groups and agencies are swamped trying to fill the need.

In the transition from child care to self-care, you need to think about several factors. Consider the age and maturity of your children and their desire to be alone. Assess their ability to follow directions and complete chores. How many children are involved and do they get along? How long will they be on their own?

Written rules, reinforced verbally, need to be posted. Can anyone visit? If so, who, how many and for how long? How should the children deal with phone calls or a stranger at the door? Can they make a check-in call? When should they call you at work? How many phone calls are permitted? Do they know what to do in case of an emergency? Are there neighbors or a relative nearby?

One step you can take to improve your children's self-care is

_____

_____.

Good child care is essential. If the children are happy, your life is easier. Your energy resources are less taxed. Secure your children. Pace your energy. You can do it.

Is Your Work Environment Healthy?

Job stress is costing this country billions of dollars annually. Equally shocking, workers' compensation claims increased about 700 percent in the past decade due to factors related to mental stress.

Nine or ten of your waking hours are spent on the job and in commuting. Feeling good about your work is important, and healthy surroundings are vital. They mediate your stress levels.

You need to take charge, to try to be in control on that first shift so you can pace your energy. You can't afford to return home fatigued.

Assess your job environment. Include physical and psychological factors. Physically, consider noise level, lighting, computer workstation, temperature and air quality.

Psychologically, think about employee morale, attitudes, sense of control and ability to adapt to organizational change. How is managerial support? Are employees recognized for their talents? Is there a good fit between your background, training and present position? How is communication? Are you happy where you are now?

NOISE POLLUTION
THREATENS HEALTH

Noise pollution threatens the health of millions of American workers. Chronic noise intensity causes physical, mental and social problems.

Focus on the noise within your immediate work area. Listen. Monitor sounds for two weeks. You may find that you are exposed to more noise than you thought.

Women are at risk for hearing problems today because they are working in larger, more open areas. Noise is intensified. Sound absorption is minimal.

For clerical workers, each workstation may have a computer, printer, telephone and typewriter, all producing irritating and stressful noise. Now multiply the workstation sounds three to nine times. Noise pollution escalates as the number of workstations multiplies. Also, women may be more sensitive to the computer's high frequency sounds, escalating their stress.

Loud noise triggers the body's fight-or-flight response. You can suffer elevated cholesterol levels, higher blood pressure, heartbeat disturbances and stomach and intestinal problems.

Reduce Noise

If possible, cut down on noise pollution. Use more sound-absorbing materials. Carpeting, draperies and bulky furniture help as buffers. Put rubber mats under computer printers, typewriters or machinery. Install soundproof cubicles that have insulation and can greatly reduce the noise level. Check if you have soundproof ceiling tiles.

When you can, move noisy equipment and machines into separate rooms away from workers. Don't try to drown out background sounds by turning up music volumes. Take frequent brief breaks away from the noise. Give your ears a rest. Avoid going from one noisy environment to another. Earplugs may be useful for some women.

The noise level in your area is:

_____ Not a problem

_____ A problem

_____ A serious problem

One step you could take to reduce the noise level is

_____

_____

LIGHTING — TOO MUCH,
TOO LITTLE?

Your workplace lighting is very important. Too little or too much can produce stress. A surface glare irritates and causes eye strain. The flickering of fluorescent lights induces fatigue and headaches.

Cool fluorescent lighting bothers some people because it has an imbalance of colors. It may be high in one color of the spectrum, yet low in others. This distortion can create eyestrain, affect energy levels and moods and cause headaches.

The use of full-spectrum lighting has increased in the workplace. This is important since many work areas today have no windows, and this lighting mimics natural sunshine without the dangerous ultraviolet rays. Full-spectrum lighting can help eye comfort and eye acuity, relaxing employees and helping them feel less fatigued.

The light in your work area is:

____ Too dim

____ Irritating

____ Good

____ Too bright

List one step you could take to improve your lighting situation.

_____

_____

YOUR COMPUTER WORKSTATION

Work space has been reduced for many mothers on the job. Private offices today are rare, obsolete or shared by several employees. Many women now work in cubicles. Noise, distractions and interruptions have escalated, increasing stress levels and co-worker conflicts. Continuous adaptation is required, and adapting drains energy resources.

Computer use has also soared. Many users of video display terminals (VDTs) are women, who are risking not only eyestrain and fatigue, but repetitive strain injuries (RSI). Some say radiation may also be a problem. You can prevent many VDT injuries and some problems.

VDT TIPS

• Use an adjustable chair. The backrest needs to support the small of the back. The seat should clear the knees. Your upper arms should be able to hang vertically with a 90-degree bend at the elbows.

• Have an adjustable keyboard. Wrists should be in a neutral position. They should not be flexed upward or downward.

• Use a footrest to support your feet and legs, if necessary. This prevents poor circulation.

• Position your monitor about 20 to 24 inches away from your eyes. Adjust the movable monitor so that the top of the screen is slightly below the horizontal line of vision. Adjust brightness and contrast to eye comfort.

• Use a copyholder next to the monitor. Make sure that both are at the same height and the same distance away. This prevents eye and neck strain.

• Secure comfortable lighting. Use about half the customary lighting in the VDT work area. Cut down on the glare from windows by using drapes, blinds or a glare screen.

• Close your eyes momentarily or gaze at distant objects to ease eyestrain and relax the eyes.

• Rather than keep your wrists and fingers poised, relax your hands on your lap or drop them to your sides when pausing.

• Take frequent, quick breaks every 20 to 30 minutes. Simple exercises that take only seconds include dropping arms to your sides and gently shaking hands and fingers. Do gentle stretches, shoulder shrugs or walk around your desk. Legislative guidelines have been enacted in several states for employees working on terminals. A VDT rest break of 15 minutes is recommended every two hours or after one hour of intense work.

One step you can take to improve your computer workstation and prevent problems is

_____

_____.

These ideas reduce not only eyestrain and fatigue problems, but also wrist, back, shoulder, and neck problems. Women are at high risk for repetitive strain injuries. One common RSI is called carpal tunnel syndrome (CTS). In this syndrome a nerve that passes through a tunnel of bone and ligament within the wrist is compressed, causing a variety of symptoms, such as tingling, numbness, aching and shooting pains.

Female computer programmers and data entry workers are not the only ones afflicted with CTS. Other vulnerable women are writers, waitresses, factory workers, upholstery workers, telephone operators, dental hygienists, bank tellers and supermarket checkout clerks.

Mothers at home who do activities that tax the fingers, hand and wrist are also at risk. Knitting or crocheting for prolonged periods of time can increase vulnerability. Some experts feel that women who are deficient in Vitamin B_6 (pyridoxine) may be more prone to CTS.

You can help to prevent carpal tunnel syndrome by being aware of its causes. Avoid continuous wrist flexion. Take frequent short breaks, and stimulate your circulation often by gently moving your arms, hands and fingers. Use good posture. Position your arms and hands so that your wrists are not strained.

If you are experiencing early signs of carpal tunnel syndrome, check with your health-care provider, and cease the repetitive movement. Avoid bending your wrist, and support your arm, wrist and hand to keep the wrist in a neutral position. Apply cool packs to soothe or reduce any inflammation.

Persistent symptoms require health-care intervention. Splints and medications may be tried. Surgery should be a last resort. Osteopathic physicians and chiropractors who specialize in musculoskeletal problems also work with carpal tunnel syndrome.

Does your job put you at high risk for repetitive strain injuries, such as carpal tunnel syndrome?

_____ Yes _____ No

List two steps you can take to prevent injuries on your job.

_____

_____

_____

TEMPERATURE MAKES THE DIFFERENCE

Have you worked in a room that was extremely hot? Have you worked in an ice-cold room? Was it difficult to function?

Extreme temperatures stress you out. Excess heat drains you of energy and causes fatigue. A hot room makes you sleepy and slows down your productivity and performance and causes you to be irritable and touchy. It also generates conflicts among co-workers.

Cold environments also decrease your ability to function. A chilly room brings discomfort, and cold temperatures constrict your blood vessels, affecting your muscles and bones. Circulation is reduced, which interferes with the coordination needed to complete assignments.

Cold impairs your concentration. You are distracted; you can't focus on tasks.

The temperature in your work area is:

_____ Cold

_____ Cool

_____ Just right

_____ Warm

_____ Hot

If temperatures are extreme, list one step you can take to improve your work area.

_____

_____

AIR QUALITY IS KEY

Working indoors can be hazardous to your health. Chemicals in construction and furnishing materials, energy-efficient buildings that are sealed against weather, and exposure to chemicals and poor ventilation systems can contribute to problems.

Women may be at higher risk for health problems because they have greater exposure to office equipment,

cleaning products, solvents and other irritants. As a result they may have a high incidence of headaches, eye, nose and throat irritations, fatigue and dizziness.

If several employees experience the same symptoms at the same time, immediate attention must be given. Report these health concerns to your supervisor. If action isn't taken and symptoms persist, contact your health department or Occupational Safety and Health Administration (OSHA).

Air quality on the job can be improved. See that stricter smoking policies are enforced. Make sure that the ventilation system is efficient, frequently cleaned and maintained and that outside fresh air is being circulated.

If you can, have copy machines and other equipment moved to separate rooms with good ventilation. Go outside during breaks and lunch hours to get fresh air and re-energize. If possible, get fresh air into your work area.

If your workstation or department is being remodeled or refurnished, check it out. Pay attention to the building materials. You have a right to know what chemicals you are being exposed to. Be alert when new carpeting or other furnishings are added.

Adorn your work area with plants, which filter and absorb harmful air pollutants. Plants that work well to purify the air include the philodendron, spider plant, golden pothos, aloe vera and corn plant. Surround yourself with greenery.

The air quality in your area is:

_____ Poor

_____ Fair

_____ Good

_____ Excellent

List one step you can take to improve your air quality.

_____

_____

Psychologically, Is Your Workplace Healthy?

Does anything drain a mother's energy faster than a negative work environment? How productive are you when morale is hitting a low or when negative attitudes are flowing through the department? Is your function affected when you are too overwhelmed to focus — too stressed to make decisions? How does anger affect employee relationships?

Several psychological health factors are key to your energy levels and workplace function. (See Figure 12.1)

Psychologically, a healthy environment increases productivity and generates energy. Because there is good communication at all levels, workplace stress is minimized and employees are motivated.

In the 1990s, organizations have been bombarded with challenges. By the time a computer system is installed and training is complete, it may be obsolete. Competition and a faltering economy have created an unstable job market. Stories about restructurings, down-sizings, buyouts, mergers, demotions and giant layoffs flood the media daily. Workers are now faced with increased workloads.

What do these rapid changes mean for you, a mother working outside the home? To survive, you need to adapt to instability. Expect _change_. Prepare for it. Get a jump on possible changes in your life. Be ahead of the game. There is no other choice.

Ask yourself three questions: (1) Are you flexible? (2) How much energy do you lose in resisting necessary changes within your department? (3) How do you view workplace change?

Continuous change is now the norm, yet this constant shifting requires you and your co-workers to move through a grieving process. Employees must work through shock, denial, anger, resistance, depression, evaluation, then varying levels of acceptance. The organizational process of change is likened to any personal loss. It takes time.

Adapting To Change

Do you resist the process? Do you defy needed policy changes or office modifications? Is your initial reaction to new ideas negative? Although resistance is part of the transition of change, watch the amount of time you expend wallowing in the struggle. Resistance siphons your energy reserve and leaves you exhausted.

To pace your first shift, and have energy for the second, you need to be flexible enough to channel your energy toward those things within your control. Take action. Make decisions. Problem-solve those elements that you can change. Write an action plan. Limit how much energy you spend on things outside your control. Give your input, but be ready to let go. You can't always control your environment.

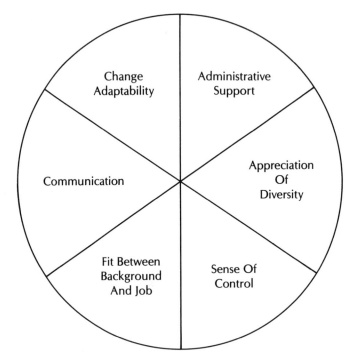

Figure 12.1. Psychological Health Factors

Your ability to be flexible is:

_____ Poor

_____ Fair

_____ Good

_____ Excellent

Could you improve on flexibility? How?

_____

_____

_____

Evaluate your perception of change. If you view change as a threat, start looking at it differently and change your attitude. Start viewing transitions as positive opportunities to grow. Accept them as challenges.

You see change at work as _____

_____

_____

Could you view these changes more positively?

_____

If yes, list some steps you could take to look at change differently.

_____

_____

_____

_____

Smart management teams minimize the stress of change. They prepare their employees and introduce transitions slowly, when possible. Employees are involved, and think-tank and brain-storming sessions are encouraged. Management coaches problem-solving by the workers, and when possible they consider employee input and solutions before implementing new ideas. Successful management provides appropriate training prior to, during and after a major change.

Support Within Your Company

Administrative support influences a mother's health, energy and productivity. Does your supervisor recognize your individual skills and talents? Do you receive feedback on completed tasks or projects? Are structured evaluations provided? Do you feel appreciated in your present position? Is there good overall communication?

Recognition

Recognition is the plus of productivity. Psychologically it energizes you. Management needs to understand the potency of acknowledging employee performance. A few words empower internal motivation. "Nice job." "Thank you." "You did a great job on the project." Be specific. A handshake and appreciation during a staff meeting or a brief memo is a powerful incentive.

Diversity

A healthy environment appreciates diversity within the department. Employees are respected for their individual uniqueness. Cultural differences are valued and viewed as assets. If personality conflicts occur, they are dealt with immediately. They are not denied, ignored or allowed to smolder and cripple productivity.

Control

Your perception of control on the job determines your stress level. If you feel you have some choices, your stress levels are lower. Mothers who feel little control have higher stress levels. They may feel helpless, and this perception negatively affects health, energy and function.

A Good Fit

The fit between your background and present position also is important psychologically and impacts your energy and stress levels. Is your educational background appropriate for your current position? Is your previous training being utilized? Are your skills, knowledge and experience a match for this job? Are your roles and responsibilities clear? Do you feel overutilized or underutilized? If there is a mismatch, you will be chronically drained of energy. Try to find your fit.

Good Communication

Communication is most important. Good communication, through all levels, connects workers and provides the energy for productivity. Poor communication stifles employee motivation and impairs performance.

Psychologically how are you doing

in your work environment? How
healthy is your department? Take this
test to evaluate your present workplace.

Check off the appropriate responses.

1. Morale is high and attitudes
   seem positive.
   _____ Yes _____ No

2. Management prepares the employees for change most of the
   time.
   _____ Yes _____ No

3. Most employees are flexible
   and view change as a necessary
   part of growth.
   _____ Yes _____ No

4. Employees feel appreciated.
   _____ Yes _____ No

5. Management recognizes employee performance and gives
   feedback.
   _____ Yes _____ No

6. The department values the diversity and contributions of the
   employees.
   _____ Yes _____ No

7. Most workers feel some control and some choice within
   this work environment.
   _____ Yes _____ No

8. Employees have a good fit between their background and
   current positions.
   _____ Yes _____ No

9. Good communication is ongoing.
   _____ Yes _____ No

10. Absenteeism is not a problem.

_____ Yes _____ No

11. The turnover rate is low.
    _____ Yes _____ No

12. Tension and stress levels are at
    a minimum.
    _____ Yes _____ No

Your answers provide a barometer
of your department. If you answered
yes to most questions, your workplace
may be psychologically healthy. If you
responded no consistently, your work
environment may be unhealthy. Your
health and energy reserves may be
threatened.

Review the factors that contributed
to the no answers. Determine if they
are chronic or temporary. Review the
chronic problems one at a time. Decide if any are within your control for
you to do something about them.

If most of the problems are un-
changeable, you may have to make a
major decision. You may have to leave
a workplace that is jeopardizing your
health, energy and performance.

List two chronic problems with
your job that the test revealed.

_____

_____

_____

If a factor is within your control,
state one step you can take to improve
your current work situation.

_____

_____

_____

Tomorrow's Workplace

The successful workplace in the future will be family sensitive. By the year 2000 two-thirds of the workers will be female. As more organizations scramble for the best and most skilled workers, they will have to care for and appreciate their employees. Negative management will be replaced. Diversity within the work environment will be valued, and employee loyalty and commitment will rebound.

The turn of the century will feature more options and flexibility for mothers. Home businesses will soar, and more mothers will choose part-time work when possible. Many women will be employed in smaller organizations. More mothers will be telecommuters — working at home on computers hooked into their workplaces.

Child care will be on-site or near-site, and family leave will be commonplace.

Education and training will be key as more jobs require college degrees and certifications. Women will switch jobs more frequently and change careers several times during their work lives. Adult education will be supported, and businesses and industries will provide basic educational skills to workers. Training will be ongoing.

Health and wellness programs will be commonplace, and lifestyle management will be rewarded. Employee assistance programs, counseling and emergency referral systems will be offered. Conscientious and informed employees will demand safer and healthier work environments.

Assess your child-care, job and work environment right now. Understand that you do have some choices. Take action. Make decisions. Your second shift needs you.

Model For Health And Energy

Pace your energy on the first shift	Ensure quality child care: ■ Safety ■ Physical and psychological health ■ Compatibility of values	Promote good self-care for older children: ■ Consider age and maturity ■ Post rules and verbally reinforce them
Assess physical work environment: ■ Noise, lighting, space ■ VDT area ■ Temperature ■ Air quality	Assess psychological factors at work: ■ Change adaptability ■ Administrative support ■ Diversity appreciation ■ Sense of control ■ Fit between background and job ■ Communication	Choose a healthy work environment to yield health and energy.

13

Safety Valves

*I use safety valves to
release pressure at work*

Are you a pressure cooker at work? Is stress getting to you? Are you afraid you might blow up at any moment? Do you feel out of control?

Slow down. Turn off the burner. Little by little, let the pressure go. Use safety valves. You can do it.

Safety valves are quick exercises you choose to do to prevent pressure build up during your workday. They buffer stress and discharge mental and physical tension. Not only do they stretch your energy resources, but they also boost energy. Try these quick techniques from head to toe.

Head, Neck And Shoulder Tension Release

HEAD TURN

Drop your head down toward your chest, pause momentarily and lift your head to a neutral position. Turn your head to the right as far as you can, as though you were looking over

145

your shoulder. Count to four. Return your head to a neutral position, looking straight ahead. Pause. Turn your head to the left as far as you can, as though you were looking over your shoulder. Count to four. Return your head to the neutral position. Pause, then repeat the sequence three more times.

ELBOW TOUCH

Clasp your hands together at the base of your skull. Bring your elbows to the front, and squeeze them together, trying to touch them. Release and return them to a neutral position. Pause for several seconds, then repeat three times.

SHOULDER SHRUG

Pull your shoulders up to your ears and hold the tension for four seconds, then gently relax your muscles and lower your shoulders. Pause. Repeat three times.

SELF-MASSAGE

Put your right hand on your left shoulder. Massage and knead the tense muscles from the shoulder, slowly across your left upper back to your neck. Reverse and use the left hand to massage the tension out of your right side.

ARM/SHOULDER ROLL

With your arms hanging loose at your sides, roll the upper arms and shoulders up, then back and in a circle six times. Pause. If you choose, for-

ward rolls can be done. Let your forearms hang loose.

How do these exercises feel? Could you feel the neck and shoulder tension releasing? Do you feel better?

List the exercise that helped you the most.

_____

_____

When are you going to start using it?

_____

_____

Eye Relaxation

Your eyes work hard during the day, and the eye muscles get tense. Whether you are on a computer or do close work, they need relief. It is crucial to relax the eye muscles periodically. Try these exercises.

DISTANT GAZE

Leave your workstation and go to the closest window. Look as far into the distance as you can. Choose the most distant object in your field of vision. Focus on it for two to three minutes. Let some of the muscles relax. This is an excellent exercise after intense close work.

EYEROLL

Close your eyes for a moment, then open them and *gently* roll them up as though you were looking at the ceiling. Hold this gaze for four seconds. Then look straight ahead.

Pause and close your eyes. Then look over to the right as far as you can. Hold that gaze. Look straight ahead. Pause and close your eyes. Then look downward as though to focus on the floor. Hold that gaze, then look straight ahead and close your eyes. Look over to the left, hold, then look straight ahead. Different eye muscles are used as you gaze in the various directions. This exercise helps break up the tension in your eye muscles.

WARM EYE RELAXATION

Rapidly rub your palms and fingers together until they are moderately warm. Close your eyes, then *gently* place the warm palms against your closed eyelids. *Do not apply pressure.* Hold this position for a minimum of one minute. Feel the warmth and relaxation. Rewarm your hands if necessary. Continue this exercise by moving the warm palms from the eyes to the sides of your head (temporal area). Massage this area in a circular motion.

Doesn't that feel good? How many exercises did you try? Did you take a moment to relax?

Write the eye exercise that felt the best.

_____

_____

_____

How often might you use this during your workday?

_____

_____

Chest, Arm, Back And Leg Relief

DEEP BREATHE

Inhale deeply through your nose. Pull the air into the lower lungs (diaphragm area). The abdomen should rise slightly. Hold for a few seconds. Pucker your lips, then slowly blow out the breath. Breathe normally several times, then repeat. Feel the tightness in your chest give way. If you work in a conspicuous area, modify this exercise by exhaling through your nostrils. This is less obvious.

SIGH

Make a big sigh through your mouth. Let out a sound of relief as the air leaves the mouth.

YAWN

Fake a yawn. Gently stretch your facial muscles. This takes in oxygen and forces the tension in your jaw and in your lower facial muscles to break up.

STRETCH

Put your arms up over your head. Imagine there is a ladder going up to the ceiling. By alternating arms, reach up and stretch as though you were trying to grab the rungs of the ladder. Reach, reach, reach, stretch, stretch, stretch, ten times. This can be done sitting or standing. It helps the back.

TENSION SHAKE

Drop your hands to your sides, then gently shake your hands and fingers. This releases tension and stimulates circulation and should be used frequently when working at a computer keyboard.

FINGER SPREAD

Spread your fingers apart as far as you can. Stretch them. Tense the muscles for five seconds. Then drop your hands to your lap and totally relax the hand and fingers. Pause, then repeat two more times.

BODY DROP

Slide your chair away from your desk. Spread your legs. (This isn't possible in a tight skirt.) Gently drop your arms, head and torso between your legs. Totally hang and relax for ten seconds. Feel the back stretch. *Caution:* Do *not* do this exercise if you have back problems. Check with your health-care provider.

BACK EXERCISE

Tighten your abdominal muscles while pushing the small of your back against your chair. Hold the tension for five seconds. Then totally relax. Repeat four times.

LEG LIFT

While sitting down, bring your legs up from the floor. Keep the knees straight. Stretch, stretch, stretch them. Then swing them rapidly for ten seconds. You can swing them together or alternate them. Drop them to the floor and relax. Repeat if desired.

If some of these techniques are awkward to do in your immediate work area, do them on your breaks. How many did you try right now?

List one technique you can start using immediately at work.

_____

_____

Commit yourself to frequently use safety valves at work. Pace your energy. Use the skills and techniques you choose at least every hour. Why not prevent the pressure build up during the day? Place a colored dot on your telephone, watch, calendar or computer monitor as a visual reminder to release the pressure.

Tell your supervisor and co-workers that you are trying some new ideas. Get them involved. Sharing increases a sense of camaraderie and improves morale and attitudes.

Safety Valves For
Mental Stress Relief

Be alert. Are you aware that you get signals when your pressure is building and is about to blow? Do you recognize the mental, emotional and behavioral signs immediately before the explosion? Do you listen? Do you act?

Many mothers share the same warnings. They might feel totally overwhelmed and out of control. They cannot concentrate or make decisions.

They are volatile — irritable, snappy, reactive and short-fused.

If these signals hit you, LISTEN and stop work immediately. Act. Remove yourself from your immediate work area. You need an instant diversion. Make it simple. Walk down the hallway and get a drink of water. Get someone to cover for you, then go to the restroom. Share a humorous moment with a colleague.

These safety valves only take a minute or two, but they release the pressure and put you back in control. Try them. Make time for them. You can do it.

Five other safety valves relieve mental stress and stabilize your work environment.

1. ALLOW YOUR LEFT BRAIN TO TAKE A MINI-VACATION

Let it slow down and relax. Imagine yourself at a favorite beach. See the waves crashing against the shoreline. Hear the seagulls. Feel the warm sun. Enjoy the imagery for two or three minutes. Even 60 seconds can work wonders. Then return to work. Your ability to concentrate will be improved.

2. IMPROVE WORKPLACE COMMUNICATION

Do your part. Communicate with honesty and directness — be assertive. Say no when yes prevents you from getting your job done. Your colleagues will have more respect for you if you are assertive.

Clarify job responsibilities, have priorities redefined, ask for help and delegate when possible. Good communication dramatically reduces employee stress.

If you are a supervisor or manager, you have a golden opportunity to model good communication. Be specific when you are instructing your employees. Be sensitive to them. Most of all, give them ongoing feedback and recognition for their accomplishments. These give workers the energy and internal motivation needed to complete mission goals successfully.

3. LEAVE YOUR WORKSTATION OVER LUNCH

Don't be a martyr and eat in. Going out relieves tension accumulated from the morning and diverts you by providing a change. The outside air energizes you, so breathe the fresh air and increased oxygen deeply. Take a brisk walk to release the stress chemicals, or run a brief errand. This change is crucial. You will be more energetic and productive the second half of the shift.

4. MAKE A WORKPLACE SUPPORT SYSTEM

Connect with other mothers who are also juggling many roles. Share ideas with them. If you have a sick child and are anxious, tell a trusted colleague. Talk on breaks and eat lunch together. Encourage your department to form a support network through social activities. A strong support system at work not only buffers stress but also prevents employee burnout.

5. TAKE A HUMOR BREAK

Keep a balance of lightness and hard work throughout your day. Humor is tops in relieving workplace stress. Some organizational giants have incorporated humor in the workplace, reaping many rewards. Playfulness training is now offered to thousands of employees every year. Most executives agree that humor is a factor in success.

What does humor do? Humor increases psychic and physical energy and boosts enthusiasm and creativity. It is a *motivational tool*. Humor improves attitudes and morale and reduces workplace panic, anxiety and worry.

Humor connects people. As one of the best communicators, it improves listening and sharing among employees, increasing teamwork. Humor enhances negotiation and compromise. It helps the group decision-making process. It is a natural in helping employee relationships.

What about your workplace? Are cartoons posted on bulletin boards, joke books in the lounge or stress-reliever toys in the breakroom? Do you share an occasional joke with a colleague? Is there an office mascot to pass around when a co-worker is down? Do staff meetings start out with something light?

Form a humor committee. Have luncheons with a humor topic. Declare a theme day. *Lighten up.*

Two mental safety valves I am going to implement in my workplace now are:

Do you use humor as a coping mechanism at work?

List one step you can take now to increase humor for yourself and co-workers.

Close Out Your Workday

As you close out your workday, remember that your energy is now at a premium. The cost is high, but you can buy it through your choices. You need to be efficient on both shifts. To be functional, you must separate your work life from your personal life.

This detachment is crucial. It needs to happen both psychologically and physically. You can't spend your second and third shifts in emotional turmoil over your first shift — then expect to return to the job fresh in the morning. This is impossible. It can't happen.

You are doing your career a grave injustice by chronic worry, anxiety and guilt at home — putting yourself down because you didn't accomplish more during the workday. Stop this energy drain. It serves no purpose, and you can't afford it.

Mothers are more productive at work if they have learned how to draw a line between their personal lives and their career lives. Leave your work at work. Don't backpack problems and drag them home at night. Your family doesn't deserve this, and you don't either.

The change and diversion on the second shift will refresh you for the next workday. Your mind and body need a break from the taxing demands at work. Don't deny them this necessary distraction. Make a commitment to switch gears and make it a total break. You need this for your health.

Three actions are necessary to preserve your sanity for the second shift.

1. Close out your workday.
2. Decompress yourself before reaching home.
3. Ease the home stampede.

Closing out your workday is accomplished in four brief steps. (See Figure 13.1)

REFLECTION

Start this step about 20 to 30 minutes before you leave the office. Now is the time to review your day. What did you accomplish? Focus on the positive — all the things you completed. Give yourself a pat on the back. Although you will want to reflect on tasks unfinished, don't put yourself down or dwell on them. Ask yourself how things went. Is there anything you learned today? As a result, will you make different decisions in the future? This step is key.

PLAN

Make decisions now. Review your unfinished projects. Write them down. (Because they are stressful, never keep mental lists.) Evaluate the importance of the tasks on your to-do list. Prioritize them. Know exactly where you are going to start tomorrow. This step is important for psychological separation because it focuses you for the next day. Now your mind is free. You can get on with your personal life.

RITUAL

Establish a ritual to separate physically from your work area. It can be any activity you choose. Some mothers clean off their entire desk. They put the files away and lock up important projects. Others turn the calendar or reorganize their workstation. Some use a checklist to close out the day. They go down the list, doing each item, such as preparing the answering machine and locking up the area. All of these activities are good ideas. They communicate that you are physically done for this shift. This is vital before leaving.

Reflection + Plan + Ritual + Self-Talk = Separation Of Work And Personal Life

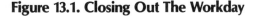

Figure 13.1. Closing Out The Workday

SELF-TALK

Now, apply firm self-talk, and make it positive. This dialogue reinforces the psychological separation that you must make in order to begin the second shift. Verbally reinforce that you are done for the day. You might use a sequence of phrases such as:

"I am finished for today."
"I did my best."
"I did a good job."
"I am a good worker."
"I didn't get everything done, but tomorrow is a new day."
"I am going to let go of my job now."
"I am going to re-energize myself through other activities."

Use some of these, all of them or make up your own. Be creative and use what works for you. Whatever phrasing you choose, repeat the same sequence every afternoon at closing.

In the evening at home, if job problems are bothering you or making you feel anxious, repeat and repeat these affirmations. You can't have your job draining you on the second shift. It isn't healthy — not for you or your job.

At night keep a notepad and pen at your bedside. If your mind triggers anxieties related to work, act on them. Jot down what you need to do in the morning. Reassure yourself with self-talk that everything is written down and that you can now go to sleep.

State one ritual you can start tomorrow to close out your workday.

Write three phrases (self-talk) you can use immediately to help you separate from work.

Decompress

You're done with your first shift. You're heading on to your second shift and you're going to need energy. Even though you are using safety valves at work to pace your energy, a time to decompress is still necessary.

Unwinding helps the transition from work to home. Whether you are picking up the children at a child-care center or going straight home, you need time alone. You need to relieve your stress, anger and tension; you need to regroup yourself after a challenging day. Don't jump from one hot spot to another.

Twenty minutes or more are needed to switch gears. If your commute is only five or ten minutes, this is not enough time. Deliberately extend your child-care time an additional 10 to 15 minutes.

Choose from a variety of unwinding activities. Go to a park and focus on the beauty. Watch the squirrels and butterflies or listen to the birds. Meditate. Do some deep breathing. Reoxygenate your lungs for renewed energy. Take a 15-minute brisk walk. Go to a store or a mall. Talk with a friend after work. *You have many choices.*

Do It In The Car

If you have a longer drive home, it is better. Take the back roads — they are less stressful. Play motivational tapes or an audiocassette of your favorite book for energy. Listen to a comedian, laugh and get in a good mood. Music is another positive mood-changer. Some mothers want upbeat music for energy after work. Others prefer soothing music to relieve stress. Use what works for you.

Keep a notebook on the passenger seat. If job worries creep in, jot down a one-word reminder . . . then let it go. Remember, you have closed out your workday. Refuse energy drains. You need every ounce of energy for that second shift.

Keep healthy snacks in your car: wheat crackers, rice cakes or bagels. Remember that your blood-sugar level can be low at the end of the afternoon. Perhaps you haven't eaten for four or five hours and you may be irritable, moody and reactive. You may have a headache or be tired. Take the time for a snack. Stabilize yourself. You will be in a better mood for the family.

Arrange with your child-care provider to give the children a snack 30 minutes before you arrive. It can make a big difference, as it reduces whining, clinging, moodiness, crying and fighting. You may have to provide the healthy snack, but it is worth it.

State one way you can decompress yourself after work.

_____

_____

Ease The Home Stampede

Arriving home can be chaotic and challenging. Children hanging on your legs and everyone talking at once can make a rough and stressful start to the second shift. *Slow down.*

Call a family conference. Choose a time when everyone is in a good mood and enlist their help. Brainstorm for ideas about making this transition smoother. Write their suggestions down. Everyone's needs must be respected. Negotiate. Compromise. Here are some ideas.

- Give all of the children a big hug, collect your hugs, then remind everyone that sharing time will be in 15 minutes.
- Spend time together as soon as you get home. Each child can have five minutes initially to share their day. They can rotate turns talking first.
- Go on a walkie-talkie. Everyone goes on a 15-minute brisk walk and talks about their day. The rewards of this are two-fold: (1) stress and tension are released and (2) this sharing can be part of family time together.
- Fix the children a snack if they didn't get one. You can change your clothes, deep breathe and gather your thoughts for the evening.
- Set a timer for 20 minutes. Regardless of age, everyone can understand that family sharing starts when the bell rings.

One step you can take to ease the home stampede is to

_____

_____

_____

If you arrive home with a headache, extreme exhaustion or illness, tell your family. Your children are very sensitive and empathic. They do understand.

Ease the home stampede. You can do it.

Model For Health And Energy

Use safety valves at work to release pressure:
- Head turn
- Shoulder shrug
- Focus eyes on distant object
- Stretch
- Leg lift/leg swing

Close out your workday:
- Reflect on the day
- Plan for tomorrow
- Establish a ritual
- Use self-talk

Be alert to signs of mental pressure and STOP work:
- Remove yourself from work area
- Get a drink of water
- Go to the restroom
- Share a light moment with a co-worker

Decompress before going home:
- Secure alone time
- Do unwinding activities
- Use music or tapes to improve mood
- Eat a healthy snack

Use mental safety valves:
- Take a mental mini-vacation
- Improve workplace communication
- Leave workstation over the lunch hour
- Secure a workplace support system
- Take a humor break

Ease the home stampede:
- Brainstorm ideas for a smooth transition
- Give and collect hugs, then share in 15 minutes
- Share upon arrival
- Go on a "walkie-talkie"

Use safety valves, decompress and ease the home stampede to yield health and energy.

14

Believe In Your Dreams

I see myself as successful

What do you want for yourself today? Tomorrow? A year from now? In your lifetime? What do you want for your children? The family? What are your needs? What do you value? Is your energy channeled toward your goals? Do you have a purpose in life?

Pause. Take time to reflect on these questions, and evaluate what is happening in your life right now.

As a mother you live in constant change. You may feel overwhelmed by the instability it creates. Uncertainty requires constant adaptation, and that takes energy.

Clarify Values And Set Goals

Clarifying values and setting goals can stabilize your life. They are driving forces and provide energy. They motivate and help you navigate life's journey.

157

Values are standards and principles you feel are so important that they become an intricate part of your belief system. You live your life by them, and your goals evolve from them.

You began to form values at birth. Your parents, relatives, peers, school and community influenced your values. In adolescence you struggled to identify and clarify them.

Your values change throughout life as your needs change. They are also altered by life experiences. Your present values are probably very different from those you had when you were a teen.

Look back. What were two distinct values from your teen years?

_____

_____

Now list two important values in your life right now.

_____

_____

Do they match? Probably not. Peer acceptance and designer clothes may have been highly valued in adolescence. Today, however, financial stability, time, health or energy may be of prime importance.

Focus on your energy level right now. How is it? Is it high or low? Are your values expressed in what you are doing? Do your activities reflect what you really want? Is there a good match between your expectations and your life right now? If not, you might feel very frustrated.

Frustration results when you are blocked from what you want. It triggers anger, and chronic anger fuels your stress level. Frustration becomes a constant energy drain and disrupts your relationships. Where are you right now?

Are your values clear to you?
_____ Yes _____ No

Do your daily activities match what you want out of life right now?
_____ Yes _____ No

Define Your Values

Evaluate yourself periodically. Reflect on the changes in your life, focusing on your values. Understand how powerfully they impact your goals. The following exercises help to clarify your present values.

EXERCISE 1

A. Read the following categories, and determine which are relevant in your life. Add others if you wish.

Self: time for self-care, grooming, stress management, personal development, good nutrition and exercise.

Children: child care, helping them study or do chores, driving them to school and extracurricular activities, attending their functions.

Significant relationship: spouse, partner.

Demands from relatives: parents, in-laws, grandparents.

Job: commuting time, hours and work brought home.

Community: professional organizations, officer commitments, support groups, religious activities, volunteer or charitable responsibilities, political involvement.

Chores: meal planning, grocery shopping, meal preparation, laundry, budgeting, housekeeping, correspondence, pet care, house and car maintenance, yard work.

Sleep: hours involved in sleep.

Social: friendships, building and maintaining a support network, social activities.

Recreational: leisure activities, hobbies, sports, fun, play, television, entertainment.

Others: _____

_____

_____

_____

B. Now, think in terms of one week (168 hours). Decide how much time you wish could be spent on each relevant segment. (See Figure 14.1)

The left circle represents the way you wish the segments were in your life. In pencil divide the whole of the circle into pie slices. Label each piece and make it clear how much time you wish you had for it. Draw each shape according to how you value it. What would be the ideal? What is really important to you?

C. Now focus on the right circle, which reflects the reality of your life. This time draw and label the pie slices the way your time is really spent.

D. Study the two circles. What do you see? Do similar segments have similar proportions? Are they different? If so, how different?

E. Identify three segments that have the greatest discrepancies between the ideal and the real. Take

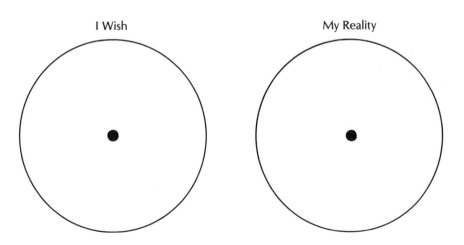

I Wish   My Reality

Figure 14.1. Value Clarification Exercise 1

your pencil and lightly shade in those segments to provide a better visual impact. It clarifies what is important to you (left circle) and what your life really looks like (right circle).

This exercise may be enlightening. As a mother you might find that, in reality, your self-nurturing activities may get squeezed out by other demands. How much time do you actually spend on your significant relationships? Sleep, also, might be less than what you value and need, or your social life might be limited or nonexistent. All of these are important. What did you find?

List the three segments that showed the greatest discrepancies.

_____

_____

_____

Circle the one you value the most. This may help you with setting goals later on.

A. Read the following list of personal values. (See Figure 14.2)

B. Rank each element (value) according to importance on a scale of 1 to 5.

How did you do? How many elements were a five (the greatest value)?

_____

_____

Choose two out of this group that are most valuable to you and list them below.

_____

_____

If you do not have these valued elements in your life, incorporate them into your future goal setting.

Take Time To Dream

Goals shape your destiny. They motivate you and provide you with vision and direction. They are the means by which your dreams are realized.

Take time to dream. Dreaming is a vital step in goal setting. Dream in the early morning before family members are awake. You are more relaxed then, and your imagination is more productive.

Project five years from now. Daydream about who or what you want to be. Allow images and ideas to float along and just enjoy being.

My recurrent daydreams center around

_____

_____

If I could have one dream come true and the resources were available, I would

_____

_____

Are Fears Blocking You?

What holds you back from realizing your dreams? Do you know? Lack of resources (money or time) often blocks mothers. But fears, however irrational, also become barriers.

On the list below decide the importance of each personal value.

Value	Lowest				Highest
	1	2	3	4	5
Accomplishment (recognition, mastery of skills, achievement, status)	___	___	___	___	___
Security (financially stable, safe home environment)	___	___	___	___	___
Intimacy (significant relationship)	___	___	___	___	___
Personal growth (mental, emotional and spiritual development, intellectual stimulation)	___	___	___	___	___
Family (health, growth and development of family members)	___	___	___	___	___
Positive job (match of skills to work, healthy environment, benefits)	___	___	___	___	___
Independence (autonomy, lack of dependence on others)	___	___	___	___	___
Time (flexibility, more options with time)	___	___	___	___	___
Creativity (chance to express yourself, play, humor, fun)	___	___	___	___	___

Figure 14.2 Value Clarification Exercise 2

Fears can immobilize and cause indecision. They lead to procrastination, and because risks are not taken, goals cannot be realized.

Fear Of Failure

Fear of failure paralyzes many mothers and puts their lives on hold. Some are irrationally terrorized by the fear of making mistakes. They deny being human and won't allow themselves to deviate from superhuman excellence. Their self-driven perfectionism fuels this fear at home and on the job.

Making mistakes, however, is part of being human. You will make mistakes. It's okay. Don't be immobilized by the fear of making them.

Failure is also human. Every genius, inventor or millionaire failed many times. Failure is not a permanent condition. It is a pause for refocusing.

Learn From Mistakes

Failure can be a powerful learning device. When one door closes in your life, another opens. Failure is essential for personal growth and development. It provides new opportunities and can be a stepping-stone to success, boosting your self-confidence.

Face The Fear Of Failure

- Give yourself *permission to be human.*
- *Move toward the fear.* Confront it. Problem-solve and believe you can work through it.
- *Refuse* to belittle yourself the next time you make a mistake.
- Use positive *self-talk.* "I can do it. I can handle it." If you make a mistake, ask yourself: "What can I learn from this?"
- Be open to failure. *View failure as a new opportunity,* not a threat.
- *Refuse to dwell* on past mistakes. Make them work for you.
- *Channel the knowledge* gained from failure toward a future success.
- Use the failure to modify or *refocus your goal.*
- Seek *professional help* or take a class if fears continue to entrap you.

Does the fear of failing or making mistakes block you from your goals?
_____ Yes _____ No

One action step you can take *now* to overcome this fear is to

_____

List two of your strengths that might help you achieve goals. Exam-

ples might be that you are persistent, determined, a go-getter, action-oriented or confident.

_____

_____

Write down two additional qualities that friends or co-workers say you have.

_____

_____

The ABCs To Successful Goals

Goals must be:
- Achievable
- Believable
- Committed to action

ACHIEVABLE

Your goals should be realistic, possible and manageable. A goal should be high enough to make you stretch, but practical in terms of money, time and energy levels.

Two additional factors are important: A goal should be specific, and you should be flexible. You may need to modify or rewrite the goal and adjust the schedule because of problems beyond your control.

BELIEVABLE

You possess a deep, inward belief that you can do it. This confident belief system has several elements. It includes a positive attitude and coaching self-talk, both of which motivate you.

Visualize Success

Visualization is crucial to your belief system. You repeatedly imagine yourself successfully achieving the goal. Daily you practice focusing on success, and you succeed in your imagination. This mental rehearsal primes you and reinforces your confidence for actual success. Mothers who are highly motivated are visionaries and see themselves as winners.

Such self-confidence enables risk-taking. Mothers who take risks believe they can make it despite adversities. They believe in their problem-solving abilities and transform difficulties into accomplishments. Without this empowering belief system, goals cannot be realized.

COMMITTED TO ACTION

This is the final step for success. Mothers committed to a goal are proactive. They take charge of their lives. They make choices and decisions. They make things happen.

Go For It

Take a few minutes and brainstorm what you would like for yourself in the next five years. Write your thoughts down. Identify some short-term and long-term goals. Short-term include daily, weekly or monthly goals. Long-term include one-year, three-year, five-year or lifetime goals.

Go back to the first value exercise. Review the discrepancies you identified. Do you want to include the one you valued most in your goal setting?

Study the second value exercise. Do you want to use those elements in your life you valued the most to set goals? Lump all your goals together. Let your mind flow, and release your dreams. List all your ideas from the first and second exercises plus new ones.

_____

_____

_____

_____

Contemplate these goals. Are they realistic or unrealistic? Consider the next five years of your life. Go back and in front of each goal write an R for realistic or a U for unrealistic. Let the U ideas go for now. Concentrate on those labeled R.

Assign the R goals into approximate six-month, two-year or five-year categories, then into personal, family or professional divisions (see chart on next page).

Is there any overlapping within the six-month, two-year and five-year goals?

If you were given six months to live, would your goals change?

Prioritize the R (realistic) goals. Which one is most important to you? Circle it so you can work on it further.

What goal is most valued by you?

_____

Why is this goal so important?

_____

Personal	Family	Professional
6 month	6 month	6 month
_____	_____	_____
_____	_____	_____
2 year	2 year	2 year
_____	_____	_____
_____	_____	_____
5 year	5 year	5 year
_____	_____	_____
_____	_____	_____

Take this goal through the following ten-step process. Remember, success happens one step at a time.

1. Write It Out

Be specific. Example: Starting November 1, I will take 30 minutes four times a week to nurture myself and become healthier.

Goal: _____

2. Brainstorm

Identify potential barriers. Do you have the resources (energy, health, time, motivation, money, support) to attain this goal? Is there anyone or anything that might block you? Write the obstacles down.

_____

_____

List ideas to work through the barriers.

_____

_____

_____

_____

Does the goal need modification at this time?

_____ Yes _____ No

If yes, rewrite the goal.

3. Set A Starting Date

Restate the date you are going to start working on this goal.

_____

_____

4. Organize By Subgoal

Identify every subgoal (activity) that is necessary to achieve the goal.

_____

_____

_____

_____

_____

_____

Number the activities in sequence. Go back and place a number at the beginning of each subgoal. What must you do first, second, third, etc.? Now rewrite the activities in the correct sequence.

(1) _____ (   )

(2) _____ (   )

(3) _____ (   )

(4) _____ (   )

(5) _____ (   )

(6) _____ (   )

Identify a realistic deadline for each activity. Place the deadline in the parenthesis after each subgoal.

5. Set A Deadline

State the deadline date by which the goal will be accomplished.

_____

6. Visualize

Visualize yourself achieving this goal. Do you believe you can succeed? Can you see yourself as successful? This step is crucial.

7. Find Support

List two support people who will help you achieve this goal.

_____

_____

External reinforcement provides coaching and encouragement and helps with problem-solving. Are there community resources that can also help?

8. Evaluate Progress

State how often you are going to evaluate goal progress (daily, weekly, monthly, annually).

_____

How will you measure goal progress?

_____

9. Reward Yourself

List a reward for achieving this goal.

_____

_____

You can also provide incentives along the way. One incentive might be a daily pat on the back for progress. Compliment yourself for taking ongoing action.

10. Write A Contract

Contracts are important for several reasons. A written commitment is a powerful motivator. Your support person can also sign it and help you evaluate your progress. Now, write in a formal commitment to the goal.

Your Contract

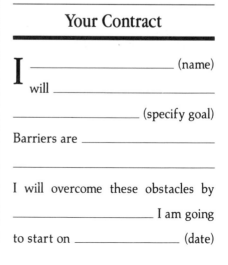

I _____ (name)
will _____
_____ (specify goal)
Barriers are _____
_____
I will overcome these obstacles by
_____ I am going
to start on _____ (date)

My main strengths are that I am

_____

_____

and _____

Activities and deadlines to accomplish

this goal are _____

_____

_____

The deadline to achieve this goal is

_____ (date)

I will visualize myself successful for

_____ minutes every day. My support

people are _____

Community resources to help me are

_____

_____

I will evaluate my goal progress every

_____ (day,

week, month, year)

I can measure my goal progress by

_____

_____

My reward for achieving this goal is

_____

_____

_____

Your signature

_____

Date

_____

Your support person's signature

_____

Date

   Make a goal checklist if you want to be sure you have covered all of the important elements. Above all, stay flexible.

   As a mother you need to reflect on where you are going in life. The how, what, when, where and why are equally important. As busy as your life is, take time to dream because your goals direct your future. If you believe in your dreams, you can achieve them.

Model For Health And Energy

Clarify your values to
stabilize your life:
- Put your energy
  toward those things you
  value

Make goals:
- Achievable
- Believable
- Committed to action

Take time to dream about
your goals

Write down realistic goals:
- Prioritize goals
- Work through barriers
- Define steps to achieve
  goals
- Set a deadline
- Visualize yourself
  achieving the goal
- Define goal support
- Evaluate goal progress
- Choose a reward

Face your fears:
- Allow yourself to be
  human
- Use mistakes or failures
  as a learning tool

Write a goal contract

Use goals to stabilize your
life to yield health and
energy.

15

Five Building Blocks To Empowerment

*I celebrate my new life
of health and energy*

others know the vital importance of health and energy.
When you have health, you have the
ability to meet the many demands of
the day. Energy is the force that
makes those commitments happen.

By now you may feel a new lease
on life, and you know you are not
alone. Millions of other mothers feel
just like you. They want the best for
themselves and their families. Health,
energy and balance help you attain
those goals.

When you understand how your
choices affect your destiny, you may
sense hope and feel more in control of
your life. If you are struggling in recovery, you understand the importance of professional help and ongoing
support. Most mothers are involved
in building or rebuilding their lives.

Building your life comes slowly, one
block at a time. Your passion to grow
and develop motivates you. You can
reach out for self-empowerment along
the way. (See Figure 15.1)

169

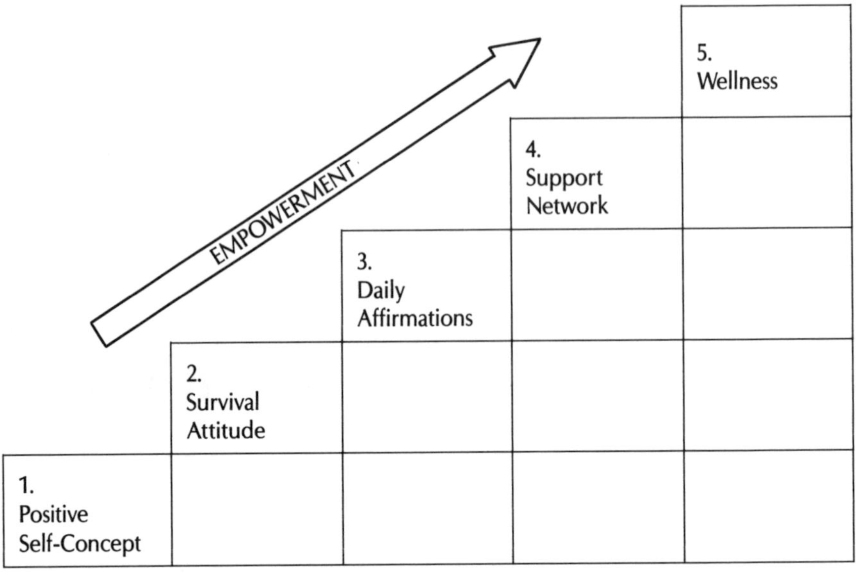

Figure 15.1. Five Building Blocks To Empowerment

Five building blocks can empower you:

- A positive self-concept
- A survival attitude
- Daily affirmations
- A support network
- Wellness

Building Block 1.
A Positive Self-Concept

A positive self-concept is the first building block for personal empowerment and is basic for you to achieve goals. Consider three components within your self-concept: self-esteem, self-image and self-confidence.

SELF-ESTEEM

Self-esteem is the foundation for all that you are and all that you can

be. Without positive self-esteem, your dreams cannot be realized.

Self-esteem refers to your belief in yourself — the conviction that you do have *value* as a human being; that you are worth something . . . as a mother . . . as a woman. You are convinced you deserve the best. It includes self-respect.

If you grew up in a dysfunctional family or were traumatized in your younger years, your self-esteem was temporarily crushed. You can, with professional help and support, work at rising above that adversity. Self-esteem can be acquired with effort and persistence.

Nurture your self-esteem through this P-L-U-S:

P = Positive thought pattern
L = Love of yourself
U = Appreciation of your Unique self
S = Self-acceptance

P — *Positive* Thought Pattern

You can take control of your thoughts. Switch negative thinking to positive, and keep your internal chatter upbeat. Refuse destructive put-downs, and limit "should" and "must" in your vocabulary.

L — *Love* Of Yourself

First, love and respect yourself. You can't be there for anyone else unless you are there for yourself. Be your own best friend and care for yourself. Reach inward and nurture yourself. This mobilizes your energy. Then you can extend yourself outward to others.

U — Appreciation Of Your *Unique* Self

Appreciate your uniqueness. There is no one like you. You are special. Your talents and skills are overflowing. Focus on what you do have. Count your blessings, and be thankful that you are you.

S — *Self*-acceptance

Accept yourself for who and what you are. Don't compare yourself to others or waste your time and energy trying to be someone else. Believe that you can change some things you don't like about yourself.

SELF-ESTEEM BOOSTERS

There are other ways to boost self-esteem. Start with easy things like your good inner qualities. For instance, you might be warm, sensitive, friendly, helpful, caring, empathic, assertive or a good listener.

Write three positive qualities you have.

_____

_____

_____

Was that difficult? Did you have trouble getting started? Did your mind go blank? Would it have been easier to write three negative qualities?

You can boost your self-esteem in many ways. Start and end each day by affirming yourself. Saying affirmations to yourself in the mirror is more powerful. Always fall asleep with a positive mind-set.

Keep a "warm fuzzy" file of positives, which might include things you've done, received or achieved. Perhaps you supported a friend during a crisis and she wrote you a special thank you. Maybe you received an outstanding evaluation at work. You may have achieved a short-term goal. The children may have given you a hand-drawn Mother's Day card.

When you are down or discouraged, pull out your file. Review it again and again and again. Immerse yourself in positive strokes. Pat yourself on the back every day of your life. Give yourself credit. You deserve it.

List one action step you can take to improve your self-esteem.

_____

_____

GOOD SELF-IMAGE

Your *self-image* is impacted by your self-esteem. If you see yourself in a bad light and think poorly of yourself, your image suffers. Your *physical and psychological perceptions* are important.

Many mothers are unhappy with their bodies. The American culture and media promote the illusion that we should have a "perfect body." Thinness continues to be in vogue. Society's message is if you can't be a size six, success cannot be yours.

Some mothers buy into and believe this destructive illusion. Their obsession leads to skipping meals and chronic dieting, which are counterproductive to health and energy.

Eating disorders, such as anorexia or bulimia can result. These disorders are more common in younger mothers, often beginning during the teen years, and they can be fatal.

The increasing number of plastic and reconstructive surgical procedures done in America is also symptomatic of the unhappiness women have with their bodies. Requests are soaring for liposuction, "tummy tucks," nose reshaping or breast augmentation or reduction. Some procedures are necessary, but mothers need to be aware of the risks involved and of their motivation.

Image also covers psychological perceptions. How do you feel and what do you think about yourself? Who are you? Do you have a sense of identity? Your self-esteem influences these perceptions.

Twirl around in front of a full-length mirror. You might be fully dressed or partially clothed. Get in touch with your thoughts, feelings and dialogue as you dance around. What are you thinking . . . what are you feeling . . . what are you saying?

Do you like the person you see in the mirror? How do you see yourself? Do you like your body, its size, pro-portions and curves? Are you focusing on imperfections? Everybody has them. Are you feeling good about yourself? Is your self-talk positive?

List two physical qualities that you like about yourself.

_____

_____

List one minor imperfection you can accept.

_____

How might you feel better about yourself? There are many ways. Scan your body in the mirror frequently with better acceptance. Visualize yourself twice a day in a more positive way. Work on areas that you choose to change. Get yourself on an exercise program.

Pamper yourself. Buy a new blouse, or restyle your hair, get a manicure or take a luxurious bath with music and candlelight. Treat yourself to a full body massage. Bathe yourself in self-acceptance.

List action steps you can take to improve your self-image.

_____

_____

_____

DEVELOP SELF-CONFIDENCE

Self-confidence evolves from a healthy self-esteem and self-image. Confidence refers to *faith in oneself*. Mothers who are confident believe they have talents and skills. They are convinced of their abilities.

Mothers with a healthy self-confidence are self-assured. They have spunk. Their confidence becomes motivational energy, and they are determined and persistent. They are risk-takers. Their tenacity leads them to success. What is your level of confidence?

My level of self-confidence is:

_____ Low
_____ Average
_____ High

Building self-confidence is the key. Start small, and increase your self-esteem and self-image first. Remember, it all starts with self-esteem — the realization that you have value. Healthy self-esteem enables a positive self-image. Those positive perceptions enable self-confidence. Self-confidence is necessary for success.

To spark confidence, make your standards, expectations and goals more realistic. Fake it until you make it. Start acting as if you are more confident. Mentally rehearse more confident behavior twice a day. Visualize yourself as more self-assured, and surround yourself with positive people.

Start with risks. Practice assertiveness, and reach for continuous challenges, growth and development. Stretch, stretch, stretch yourself.

List one step you can take to increase your self-confidence.

_____

_____

Your self-esteem, image and confidence impact your children and the level of family energy. If you feel better about yourself, they will, too. Positive behaviors are contagious. They rub off.

Remember, you are the coach in your children's lives. Do everything you can to foster their self-esteem. Relationships are more positive when individuals have high levels of self-confidence.

A positive self-concept is your first building block for empowerment. Now reach for the second building block.

Building Block 2.
A Survival Attitude

A survival attitude is the second building block to personal empowerment. Shape an attitude to survive. If you have an "I can do it" frame of mind now, resiliency to stress and psychological hardiness strengthen that mood.

Inner Strength

Mothers who survive believe in their inner strength. They know that if they fall down, they can get back up. They bounce back in hard times.

Resourcefulness

In a crisis survivors have confidence in their problem-solving skills. They are resourceful and ask for help, viewing this as a sign of strength, not weakness.

Optimism

Successful mothers are optimists. They use their optimism as energy . . . a moving force. They twist negatives into positives and push forward to success. They use their optimistic energy to mediate their stress level and prevent motherhood burnout.

HARDY MOTHERS

Hardy mothers have three unique qualities: *commitment, challenge* and *control.* They are committed to their families and to themselves. They are involved with their careers, yet they have the capacity to separate their work from their personal lives.

Mothers who believe in their own personal growth and development are hardy. Their learning is ongoing. They are *committed* to a healthy balance in their lives, and they pace themselves throughout the day, replenishing their energy stores daily. They are convinced that their lives have meaning and value.

Hardy mothers see change as a *challenge.* They welcome it as an opportunity for growth. They ride the roller coaster of life with finesse, and bumps along the way don't throw them. When they are down, they know there is just one way to go, up.

Mothers who are hardy also have a sense of *control* over their lives. They accept responsibility for the choices they make and believe they can shape their destiny through those choices. Are you hardy?

I feel a strong commitment to what I am doing in my life.

_____ Yes   _____ No

I see change in my life as a challenge.

_____ Yes   _____ No

I have a sense of control over my life and accept responsibility for the choices I make.

_____ Yes   _____ No

If you answered no to two or three of the questions, evaluate how you might change your attitude and perception.

Hardiness can be learned. Get involved in your life, and work at developing a positive attitude. Let your life toughen you. Very few mothers are born survivors. Start accepting change as a challenge. Start believing you do have choices. It takes time, but you can do it.

List one step you can take to become more hardy.

A survival attitude is the second building block for empowerment. Now reach for the third building block.

Building Block 3.
Affirmations For Reinforcement

Affirmations empower many mothers and are the third building block for personal empowerment. Affirmations provide inner energy and personal power. They coach and encourage you. They lift you up when you are down and make life manageable. Use them to survive impossible days.

You can write your own affirmations and make your own tape. If you are uneasy with your voice, have a friend with a soothing, encouraging voice record them for you.

Begin and end each day of your life affirming yourself. At bedtime use affirmations as you drift into quality sleep. In the morning set your alarm ten minutes early and immerse yourself in empowerment. You might play your tape while you are getting ready to start your busy day on the run.

Here are a few examples of affirmations for different areas of your life. Make up your own.

SELF-ENCOURAGEMENT

I am unique. I am a special person.

I believe in myself and my potential.

I accept myself for who I am, knowing that I can change some things that bother me.

This is a new day for me.

I have choices. I choose to take one day at a time.

FAMILY

I appreciate the uniqueness of each child.

Our family can handle challenges.

We are survivors. We are going to be okay. We will make it.

We support each other in growth and development.

MENTAL/EMOTIONAL/ SPIRITUAL/PHYSICAL

I limit worry and guilt.

I am in charge of my stress reaction.

I choose a positive attitude.

I release my anger constructively.

I move toward my goal without fear.

I pull on the strength of a Higher Power.

I choose a healthy lifestyle.

I take time to replenish my energy pool each day.

I release my physical tension.

SOCIAL

I surround myself with positive people.

I choose healthy relationships.

I assert myself to protect my health and energy.

I keep a strong support network.

WORK

I am one person. I am human. I can only do one thing at a time.

I see changes at work as opportunities.

I respect the diversity of my co-workers.

I communicate assertively.

I take frequent mini-breaks throughout the day to pace my energy and balance out my hard work.

Affirmations do not replace the need to take action and solve problems. They simply remind you that you have the inner power to be in charge of your life.

Write one affirmation from any group that you find empowering.

_____

_____

_____

When will you start using it?

_____

Affirmations are your third building block for empowerment. Now reach for the fourth building block.

Building Block 4.
A Support Network

A support system strengthens mothers and is the fourth building block for personal empowerment. It creates energy, it is life-giving. It mediates stress levels and prevents burnout. This external boost becomes a lifeline to mothers challenged in a complex world. Mothers with a strong support network are healthier.

Support people coach and encourage you in both your work and personal lives. They are cheerleaders and provide external motivation. They can gently nudge you along as you achieve goals or survive a crisis.

Sadly, mothers on the run often fail to keep their support system, the very substance that keeps them functional.

Consider your present support network, including personal, family, community and work connections. The number of support persons or groups isn't the most significant factor. The quality of the relationships is more important. Where do you stand?

Read each of the following categories. After each description, stop and fill in your network.

PERSONAL SUPPORT

Your spouse or significant partner can be a big part of your network. This person may nurture you and share responsibilities in the home. Your children are also important to you. They are sensitive and may bolster you with hugs or encouraging comments. Your pet may be a good listener and relieve your stress.

An exceptional friendship can also be included. This friend may have stuck by you through thick and thin, and you might call her first in a crisis.

STOP! Fill in your personal network now. Include the most important individuals in your life. (See Figure 15.2)

FAMILY SUPPORT

Other family members are also part of your support network. Mother, father, siblings, grandparents, aunts, uncles and cousins are possibilities. You may not have any relatives living nearby, but you receive their support from letters and telephone calls.

Neighbors or friends may be surrogate family members and can be part of this support category.

STOP! Fill in the family grouping now.

COMMUNITY SUPPORT

Individuals and groups in the community add to your network of support. Your children's teachers, school and PTA friendships may offer support. You might have backing if you have attended classes at the community college, university or vocational center.

Professionals or groups in your life may be a big part of this network. Therapists, counselors, physicians, nurses and health resources offer support. Parenting agencies or groups can be helpful. Clergy (minister, priest or rabbi) or other spiritual leaders may provide assistance. Religious groups and activities can lend support, too.

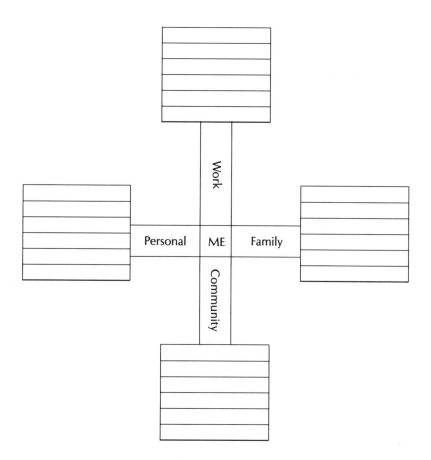

Figure 15.2. Support Network Exercise

Self-help or support groups can be part of your lifeline. These groups provide hope, empowerment and a mechanism for personal recovery, growth and development. (See Appendix for a state-by-state self-help clearinghouse list that can connect you with an appropriate self-help group.) Other groups related to your hobbies and recreational activities may give you support.

Stop and fill in your community support now.

WORK SUPPORT

Co-workers can be a link to survival. Your supervisor or administrator may also lend support. Work-related activities or groups may be a significant part of your network. Include career groups or your professional organization.

Stop and fill in your work component now.

Study all four areas. Don't be surprised if your network is small. If you grew up in a dysfunctional family, your family support may be minimal or nonexistent. It's okay. You can build on what you have.

Now define the value of the relationships. Place letters in front of each person or group. Put a CQ for the Closest and highest Quality relationships; an S for Supportive, yet not as close and high quality; and a DS for Distant Support, those still in your life, but not active.

Now, go back to all of those labeled CQ.

List the names and phone numbers of the three most significant and supportive people or groups in your life. Who would you call in a crisis? Who would see you through hard times?

Name   Phone #

_____   _____

_____   _____

_____   _____

Rate your support system now. How do you view your network? Check one:

_____ Poor

_____ Fair

_____ Good

_____ Very good

_____ Excellent

If, for any reason, you circled poor or fair, list one step you can take to build your support network.

_____

_____

_____

THE MALE IN YOUR LIFE

Your spouse or significant partner can be an important part of your life. This relationship can offer lifeline strength as he provides love, caring, intimacy and energy.

Complete the following checklist on the male in your life. Score yourself from 1 to 5 using the following key:

1 = Strongly Disagree

2 = Somewhat Disagree

3 = Agree

4 = Moderately Agree

5 = Strongly Agree

_____ He accepts me as I am. He does not try to control me. He does not try to change me to fit his expectations.

_____ He energizes me. When I am with him, I feel good.

_____ He respects me. He treats me well. He values my intelligence, judgment and decisions.

_____ We discuss parenting styles and discipline differences away from the children.

_____ He is a good listener. Our communication is good. He believes in negotiation and compromise.

_____ He helps me with the house and children. He believes in family teamwork.

_____ He respects my sexual needs and feelings.

_____ He has a good sense of humor. He believes in playfulness to balance hard work.

Scoring: If you scored 32 to 40, you may have an excellent relationship. If you scored 24 to 31, you may have a good relationship. If you scored under 24, decide to what degree there may be a problem with your relationship.

Review any questions you answered with a 1. Think about why this is such a problem and how this could be different.

The male in my life and I have a _____ relationship.

If your response was negative, list one beginning step you could take to deal with this concern.

_____

_____

_____

The male in your life can make the difference between your running on energy or running on empty. If you have a wonderful relationship, count your blessings.

Some relationships can be chronically draining and take every ounce of energy you have. You can't afford this as a mother. If you are in an abusive, traumatic or negative relationship, you need to make some decisions. Your health and sanity are at stake.

Seek professional help: psychologists, therapists, mediators or family counselors. Reach out for self-help and support groups to empower you and help you along the way.

If you are recently separated or divorced, you may still be grieving. Grieving takes time and energy. Recovery happens one step at a time.

Be extra good to yourself. Pamper yourself and pull on your support net-

work. Allow time to work through your intense emotions and feelings. Slowly build your self-esteem and try to reorganize and rebuild your life.

You need to re-establish your identity and roles and shape new traditions for you and your children. Be empathic with your children because they are also grieving. They need extra love, hugs and understanding just as you do. Give them time to work through this transition.

List one step you can take to improve your relationship with the man in your life.

_____

_____

A good support network is your fourth building block for empowerment. Now reach for the fifth building block.

Building Block 5. Wellness

Wellness is the fifth and final building block for personal empowerment. A choice for wellness means a choice for health and energy. How can you move ahead or reach for goals without health and energy?

Wellness is a lifestyle chosen for optimal functioning. A state of well-being empowers and strengthens you, and channels your energy toward balance and quality of life. Wellness gives you energy that helps you reach your highest potential.

A state of wellness encompasses all areas of your life: health, family, social, career, financial, safety and environment. You want all of these areas to do well.

To simplify, focus on four dimensions: *health, family and social, environmental* and *occupational*. Programs for wellness are soaring in some organizations, promoting health, emphasizing illness prevention. Businesses and industries are finding improved morale, increased productivity and lowered health-care costs.

CHECK YOUR WELLNESS LEVEL

Read the following wellness qualities. Check off those characteristics that you have.

Health (mental, emotional, spiritual and physical):

_____ Ongoing stress management for you and the family

_____ Intellectual striving and personal growth and development

_____ High self-esteem, assertiveness and a positive attitude

_____ Healthy emotions (constructive outlets for anger)

_____ Positive spiritual dimension (philosophy of life, belief system, values, goals)

_____ Humor, fun, play and leisure activities

_____ Good nutrition and exercise program

_____ Regular health screening (physical workup, vaccinations)

_____ Self-care: monthly breast self-exam, skin monitoring, AIDS prevention, back problem prevention

_____ Eye and dental care

_____ Emergency skills (CPR, first aid)

_____ Drug validation (prescription and over-the-counter drugs)

_____ Nonsmoker and limits alcohol

_____ Quality sleep and breaks to replenish energy stores

Rate your health dimension of wellness. Check one.

_____ Poor

_____ Fair

_____ Good

_____ Very good

_____ Excellent

List one step you can take to improve your health dimension.

_____

_____

FAMILY AND SOCIAL WELLNESS

Check those you presently have.

_____ Healthy lifestyle and relationships within the family

_____ Safe and healthy child care

_____ Shared chores — family teamwork

_____ Good communication, family meetings, daily hugs

_____ Realistic time management, good financial management

_____ Use of parenting resources

_____ Solid support system — network also outside the family

_____ Safe and healthy sexual lifestyle

Rate your family and social dimension of wellness. Check one.

_____ Poor

_____ Fair

_____ Good

_____ Very good

_____ Excellent

List one step you can take to improve your family and social wellness.

_____

_____

ENVIRONMENTAL WELLNESS

Check those you presently have.

_____ Safety at home — poisons and toxic substances locked up and emergency numbers known

_____ Good food supply — home or organically grown, limited processed foods

_____ Air, water, ground awareness and safety — well water tested annually

_____ Safety on the road — buckled seatbelt, traffic rules obeyed, choosing not to drive under the influence of alcohol/drugs

_____ Recycling participation

Rate your environmental dimension of wellness. Check one.

_____ Poor

_____ Fair

_____ Good

_____ Very good

_____ Excellent

List one step you can take to improve your environmental wellness.

_____

_____

_____

OCCUPATIONAL WELLNESS

Check those you presently have.

_____ Safe workplace environment — labeling of harmful substances and appropriate training of employees

_____ Healthy environment — quality air, good ventilation, controlled noise, comfortable temperature and lighting

_____ Good match of your background, experience and job role

_____ Supportive administration — ongoing employee respect, feedback and recognition

_____ Good communication throughout all levels

_____ Strong co-worker support system

Rate your occupational dimension of wellness. Check one.

_____ Poor

_____ Fair

_____ Good

_____ Very good

_____ Excellent

List some steps you can take to improve your occupational wellness.

_____

_____

_____

_____

_____

_____

Treasure Your Health And Energy

If you have good health, give thanks every day, and continue to protect your health and secure your energy. If you have health problems, take every measure to prevent further progression.

Make lifestyle changes for a healthier and more energetic you. Prevent health problems.

Take care of yourself as a mother. If you don't guard your health and energy, no one else will. Your health is your life and your energy. Stretch yourself for wellness, and strive for a healthier you.

You can take charge of your life. Nurture yourself . . . the rest will follow. You can do it.

Model For Health And Energy

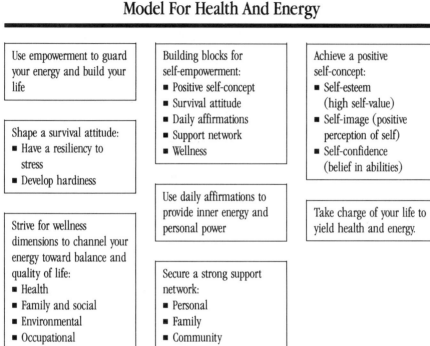

Use empowerment to guard your energy and build your life

Shape a survival attitude:
- Have a resiliency to stress
- Develop hardiness

Strive for wellness dimensions to channel your energy toward balance and quality of life:
- Health
- Family and social
- Environmental
- Occupational

Building blocks for self-empowerment:
- Positive self-concept
- Survival attitude
- Daily affirmations
- Support network
- Wellness

Use daily affirmations to provide inner energy and personal power

Secure a strong support network:
- Personal
- Family
- Community
- Work

Achieve a positive self-concept:
- Self-esteem (high self-value)
- Self-image (positive perception of self)
- Self-confidence (belief in abilities)

Take charge of your life to yield health and energy.

APPENDIX

SELF-HELP CLEARINGHOUSES IN THE UNITED STATES

Self-help is a process whereby people who share common concerns help one another to cope more effectively. It is a peer-to-peer process. If you are going through major life changes, have an addiction or have a mental or physical problem, it may be helpful for you to be with others who share your concern. If a family member or friend has a specific problem, you can be helped, too. Call your state self-help clearinghouse and connect with the appropriate self-help group.

California*	1-800-222-LINK (in CA only) — administrative, call (310) 825-1799
Connecticut	(203) 789-7645
Illinois*	(708) 328-0470 — administrative, call (708) 328-0471
Iowa	1-800-952-4777 (in Iowa) — (515) 576-5870
Kansas	1-800-445-0116 (in Kansas) — (316) 689-3843

Massachusetts	(413) 545-2313
Michigan*	1-800-777-5556
Minnesota	(612) 224-1133
Missouri	
Kansas City	(816) 472-HELP
St. Louis	(314) 773-1399
Nebraska	(402) 476-9668
New Jersey	1-800-FOR-M.A.S.H.
New York	
Brooklyn	(718) 875-1420
Westchester**	(914) 949-6301
North Carolina	
Mecklenberg area	(704) 331-9500
Ohio	
Dayton area	(513) 225-3004
Toledo area	(419) 475-4449
Oregon	
Portland area	(503) 222-5555
Pennsylvania	
Pittsburgh area	(412) 261-5363
Scranton area	(717) 961-1234
South Carolina	
Midlands area	(803) 791-9227
Tennessee	
Knoxville area	(615) 584-6736

Memphis area   (901) 323-0633

Texas*   (512) 454-3706

Greater   (703) 941-LINK
Washington, DC

* Maintains listings of additional local clearinghouses operating within that state.
** Call Westchester only for referral to local clearinghouses in upstate New York.

For national U.S. listings and directories:

American Self-Help Clearinghouse
(201) 625-7101, 625-9053

National Self-Help Clearinghouse
(212) 642-2944

REFERENCES AND RECOMMENDED READINGS

Ackerman, R.J. **Perfect Daughters.** Deerfield Beach, FL: Health Communications, 1989.

Atkinson, H. **Women And Fatigue.** New York: Pocket Books, 1985.

Bach, G. and Torbet, L. **The Inner Enemy: How To Fight Fair With Yourself.** New York: Berkley Books, 1983.

Benson, H. **Beyond The Relaxation Response.** New York: Berkley Books, 1984.

Blanchard, M. and Tager, M.J. **Working Well: Managing For Health And High Performance.** New York: Simon and Schuster, 1985.

Bluestein, J. **Parents, Teens And Boundaries: How To Draw The Line.** Deerfield Beach, FL: Health Communications, 1993.

Bradshaw, J. **Bradshaw On: The Family.** Deerfield Beach, FL: Health Communications, 1988.

Braiker, H.B. **The Type E Woman.** New York: A Signet Book, 1986.

Branden, N. **The Power Of Self-Esteem.** Deerfield Beach, FL: Health Communications, 1992.

Burns, D. **The Feeling Good Handbook.** New York: Plume Book, 1989.

Cancer Facts & Figures — 1992. Atlanta, GA: American Cancer Society, Inc., 1992.

Cousins, N. **Anatomy Of An Illness.** New York: Bantam Books, 1979.

Curran, D. **Stress And The Healthy Family.** Minneapolis, MN: Winston Press, 1985.

DeFoore, B. **Anger: Deal With It, Heal With It, Stop It From Killing You.** Deerfield Beach, FL: Health Communications, 1991.

Dowling, C. **Perfect Women.** New York: Summit Books, 1988.

Dyer, W. **What Do You Really Want For Your Children?** New York: William Morrow and Company, Inc., 1985.

Eliot, R.S. and Breo, D.L. **Is It Worth Dying For?** New York: Bantam Books, 1984.

Feltman, J., Ed. **Prevention's Giant Book Of Health Facts: The Ultimate Reference For Personal Health.** Emmaus, PA: Rodale Press, 1991.

Fishel, R. **Healing Energy.** Deerfield Beach, FL: Health Communications, 1991.

Freudenberger, H. and North, G. **Women's Burnout.** New York: Penguin Books, 1985.

Friedman, M. and Ulmer, D. **Treating Type A Behavior And Your Heart.** New York: Fawcett Crest, 1984.

Girdano, D.A., Everly, Jr., G.S. and Dusek, D.E. **Controlling Stress And Tension.** Englewood Cliffs, NJ: Prentice Hall, 1986, 1990.

Gold, M. **The Good News About Depression.** New York: Villard Books, 1986.

Greenberg, J. **Managing Stress: A Personal Guide.** Dubuque, Iowa: Wm. C. Brown, 1984.

Hanson, P. **Stress For Success.** New York: Doubleday, 1989.

Hauri, P. **The Sleep Disorders.** Kalamazoo, MI: Upjohn, 1982.

Helmstetter, S. **The Self-Talk Solution.** New York: Pocket Books, 1987.

Helmstetter, S. **What To Say When You Talk To Yourself.** New York: Pocket Books, 1986.

Hyatt, C. and Gottlieb, L. **When Smart People Fail.** New York: Penguin Books, 1987.

Kellogg, T. and Harrison, M. **Finding Balance.** Deerfield Beach, FL: Health Communications, 1991.

Kirsta, A. **The Book Of Stress Survival.** New York: Fireside Book, 1986.

Kushner, M. **The Light Touch: How To Use Humor For Business Success.** New York: Simon and Schuster, 1990.

Lakein, A. **How To Get Control Of Your Time And Your Life.** New York: Signet Books, 1973.

Leman, K. **Bonkers: Why Women Get Stressed Out And What They Can Do About It.** Old Tappan, NJ: Fleming H. Revell Company, 1987.

Lerner, H. **The Dance Of Anger.** New York: Harper & Row, 1985.

Loehr, J.E. and Migdow, J.A. **Take A Deep Breath.** New York: Villard Books, 1986.

Michigan Department of Public Health, Center for Health Promotion. **Basic Nutrition Facts: A Nutrition Reference.** East Lansing, MI: Cooperative Extension Service, Michigan State University, 1989.

Nathan, R.G., Staats, T.E. and Rosch, P.J. **The Doctors' Guide To Instant Stress Relief.** New York: G.P. Putnam's Sons, 1987.

Norris, G. and Miller, J. **The Working Mother's Complete Handbook.** New York: Plume Book, 1979, 1984.

Null, G. **Change Your Life Now: Get Out Of Your Head, Get Into Your Life.** Deerfield Beach, FL: Health Communications, 1993.

Pearsall, P. **Super Immunity.** New York: Fawcett Gold Medal, 1987.

Pelletier, K. **Healthy People In Unhealthy Places.** New York: Merloyd Lawrence Book, 1984

Pines, A. and Aronson, E. **Career Burnout.** New York: The Free Press, 1988.

Podell, R. **Doctor, Why Am I So Tired?** New York: Pharos Books, 1987.

Procaccini, J. and Kiefaber, M. **Parent Burnout.** New York: Signet Books, 1983.

Robinson, B. **Stressed Out?** Deerfield Beach, FL: Health Communications, 1991.

Rosenthal, N. **Seasons Of The Mind.** New York: Bantam Books, 1989.

Ryan, R.S. and Travis, J.W. **The Wellness Workbook.** Berkeley, CA: Ten Speed Press, 1981.

Schafer, W. **Stress Management For Wellness.** New York: Holt, Rinehart and Winston, 1987.

Schauss, A. **Nutrition And Behavior.** New Canaan, CT: Keats Publishing, Inc., 1985.

Shaevitz, M. **The Superwoman Syndrome.** New York: Warner Books, 1984.

Shaffer, M. **Life After Stress.** Chicago, IL: Contemporary Books, Inc., 1983.

Silent Epidemic: The Truth About Women and Heart Disease. Dallas, TX: American Heart Association, 1989.

Smith, A.W. **Overcoming Perfectionism.** Deerfield Beach, FL: Health Communications, 1990.

Smith, M. **When I Say No, I Feel Guilty.** New York: The Dial Press, 1975.

Stearns, A. **Coming Back.** New York: Ballantine Books, 1988.

Stellman, J. and Henifin, M.S. **Office Work Can Be Dangerous To Your Health.** New York: Pantheon Books, 1983.

Tannen, D. **You Just Don't Understand.** New York: Ballantine Books, 1990.

Vedral, J. **My Teenager Is Driving Me Crazy.** New York: Ballantine Books, 1989.

Waitley, D. **Being The Best.** New York: Pocket Books, 1987.

Wegscheider-Cruse, S. **Learning To Love Yourself.** Deerfield Beach, FL: Health Communications, 1987.

Wills-Brandon, C. **Learning To Say No.** Deerfield Beach, FL: Health Communications, 1990.

Witkin-Lanoil, G. **The Female Stress Syndrome.** New York: Berkley Books, 1984.

Important Books for Mothers
from Health Communications

DAILY AFFIRMATIONS FOR PARENTS: How to Nurture Your Children
And Renew Yourself During The Ups And Downs Of Parenthood
Tian Dayton

If you're taking care of children and trying to care for yourself too, you deserve
encouragement and loving ideas for keeping everyone's needs in perspective.
Code 151-8 .... $6.95

PEACEFUL PREGNANCY MEDITATIONS: A Diary For Expectant Mothers
Lisa Steele George

Affirmations for every day you're expecting cover the joys and fears of pregnancy.
There's room to record your own feelings on each page.
Code 2638 .... $9.95

PARENTS, TEENS AND BOUNDARIES: How to Draw The Line
Jane Bluestein, Ph.D.

You can enjoy your children's teenage years if you know how to set boundaries and
make them stick. Twenty firm yet loving ways to deal with teens that really work.
Code 2794 .... $8.95

THE SUPERMARKET DIET: How Food Labels Can Help
You Eat Healthfully And Control Your Weight
Valerie George, Ph.D. and Richard N. Nathanson

Keep your family healthy and control your weight with ordinary supermarket
foods. Easy tips for nutritious shopping, food plans, menus and recipes.
Code 2611 .... $9.95

HOW TO TURN YOUR MONEY LIFE AROUND: The Money Book For Women
Ruth Hayden

Feelings of fear and shame about money keep many women from taking charge of
their finances. Help for developing appropriate attitudes and useful money skills.
Code 2255 .... $9.95

CHICKEN SOUP FOR THE SOUL
101 Stories to Open The Heart And Rekindle The Spirit
Jack Canfield and Mark Victor Hansen

Here is a treasury of 101 stories collected by two of America's best-loved inspira-
tional speakers. Put a smile in your heart and share it with your family.
Code 262X $12.00

3201 S.W. 15th Street
Deerfield Beach, FL 33442-8190
1-800-851-9100

**Health
Communications, Inc.**